D1176985

FLORIDA HIKING TRAILS

The Official Guide to the Florida Trail on Public Lands

based on *Walking the Florida Trail*
by
John M. Keller and Ernest A. Baldini

Edited by Nancy B. and Susan K. Gildersleeve

Maupin House
Gainesville, Florida
1991

Library of Congress Cataloging-in-Publication Data

Florida Hiking Trails: The Official Guide to the Florida Trail on Public Lands. / Edited by Nancy B. Gildersleeve and Susan K. Gildersleeve.--1st. ed.
172pp. cm.
Includes index, bibliography
ISBN-0-929895-08-8
1. Hiking--Florida--Florida Trail--Guide-books. 2. Florida Trail (Fla.)--Description and travel--Guide-books. I. Gildersleeve, Nancy B., 1939– . II. Gildersleeve, Susan K., 1967– .
GV199.42.F6F56   1991
917.59'04--dc20   91-14257
                                                              CIP

First edition. Printed in the United States of America
Typeset by Susan K. Gildersleeve
Graphic design and production by Audrey S. Wynne
Cover photograph by John Moran
Back cover photograph by James A. Kern
Illustrations by Arthur P. Ives and John M. Keller
Cartography by Ernest A. Baldini assisted by N. Dean Palmer, Richard McCurdy, Frank Orser and Nancy B. Gildersleeve on maps under copyright by the Florida Department of Transportation.

This official trail guide is available from the Florida Trail Association, P.O. Box 13708, Gainesville, Florida 32604, or from Maupin House Publishing, P.O. Box 90148, Gainesville Florida 32607.

DISCLAIMER
The Florida Trail Association, Inc. proclaims the information contained in this guide to be correct at the time of publication and assumes no liability arising from the use of this information.

Editor's Note:

Running up the center of the state, remote yet accessible, the Florida Trail passes ancient live oaks, cypress, wild azaleas on ravines, giant palmettos and pine. Hikers see rare plants, deer, countless birds and many small animals. Remnants of pioneer Florida and examples of modern agriculture border the trail.

I write this in the noisy city after a three-day walk through the Ocala Forest, where we slept through a thunderstorm, cooled tired feet in a spring, listened to sandhill cranes on a prairie in early morning, and walked on bright sand in the moonlight. The Florida trail is a special place. This guide will open it to the public.

Preparing this book was a great group effort. Thanks are due to the FTA section leaders responsible for individual trails and especially to:

Frank Orser, FTA VP for Trails, whose steadfast encouragement and long hours of help with trail data and maps kept the project on track as the months went by;

Art Ives and John Keller who prepared special trail drawings and Jim Kern, who took the photographs which so enhance the book;

Ernie Baldini, FTA cartographer for many years, who taught us the computer program for trail data and helped us prepare maps;

Susan Gildersleeve, who spent long hours at the terminal, learned two new computer programs, prepared a manuscript from sometimes unreadable copy, and still managed to graduate from college;

Judy Trotta, FTA office manager, whose help with the computer and assistance with gathering and checking data was invaluable.

To all my hiking buddies, past, present and future, thanks for waiting while I checked out what was "just around the next bend." I hope this book will bring the quiet pleasures of outdoor Florida to others seeking an escape from its expanding population.

Nancy B. Gildersleeve
Gainesville, Florida
July 1991

Acknowledgements

Florida is really the winter hiking capital of the United States with many miles of trails. The Florida Trail Association has worked with both public and private agencies to develop trails and make them available to the public. After building these trails we felt the need to find a way to let others know about them. This guide was written to make the hiking trail information available to the general public.

We are indebted to the volunteers, led by Nancy Gildersleeve, who have given up their evenings, weekends and holidays to prepare this book for publication.

Paul Cummings
Florida Trail Association
President

Appreciation is extended to these property owners and managers for their support in the development and maintenance of the Florida Trail:

U.S. Dept. of Agriculture - Forest Service
U.S. Dept. of the Interior - National Park Service
U.S. Dept. of the Interior - Fish and Wildlife Service
U.S. Army Corps of Engineers
U.S. Air Force
FL Dept. of Natural Resources - Division of Recreation & Parks
FL Game and Fresh Water Fish Commission
FL Dept. of Agriculture & Consumer Services - Division of Forestry
South Florida Water Management District
Southwest Florida Water Management District
St. Johns River Water Management District
Suwannee River Water Management District

Table of Contents

This book is dedicated to the volunteers of the
Florida Trail Association who since 1964 have
given time and energy to make hiking trails
available to the people of Florida.

The Florida Trail on Public Lands, 1991

INTRODUCTION

The Trail System
The Florida Trail System consists of linear and loop hiking trails located throughout Florida. It passes through some of the most scenic areas of the state. Thirty to seventy mile segments of the trail are located on public land in Big Cypress National Preserve, around Lake Okeechobee, in the Withlacoochee, Ocala, Osceola, and Appalachicola Forests, and in the St. Marks National Wildlife Refuge. At present, these are connected by trails on private lands and forest roads. The goal is a continuous footpath of 1,300 miles to be designated the Florida National Scenic Trail.

The system was developed by the Florida Trail Association (FTA) and is maintained by its members. The Association began with 24 members in 1966 and now has more than 5,000 members. Its founder, Jim Kern, also co-founded the American Hiking Society. Almost all of the clearing and marking of the trail was done using volunteer labor and contributions.

Use of the Trail
There are some hiking trails which connect to trails listed in this book that are on private land and can only be used by members of the Florida Trail Association. Please detour around these areas. Failure to comply with this requirement can subject the hiker to prosecution under Florida's very strict trespassing laws.

About this Guidebook
This book is the first public guide to the Florida Trail. Earlier editions of this book titled *Walking the Florida Trail* have been published for the exclusive use of Florida Trail Association members and contain information about the hiking trails in Florida on private land which are open to FTA members only. For information on FTA membership, see page 166.

The Florida Trail is divided into regions corresponding to the state's four geographical areas. These regions are subdivided into trail sections and these are described and mapped in this book. The maps are based on county maps from the Florida Department of Transportation maps or on the more detailed topographic maps of the U. S. Geological Survey.

The descriptive material about the trails, flora and fauna in this guide was compiled by the members of the FTA or drawn from state publications. A bibliography is provided to help you gather additional information. The Association hopes this book will stimulate interest in outdoor Florida and lead hikers to discover more about it.

It is important that the reader understand the limitations of this guidebook. When trail conditions change, the routes may be changed. Some trail sections may be closed. The FTA, the land manager or the owner will use signs to notify the hiker, and blazes will be changed. Trail status reports are available from the FTA or the public agency involved. Hikers who use this guide on the trail are encouraged to report significant errors or confusing directions to the FTA or the land manager involved. *When in doubt, follow the blazes!*

General Description, Data, Maps, and Scale

Each section in the Florida Trail system is presented in this guide with general information, trail head location, a page of mileage data and a map or maps. The type of hiking, water availability, parking suggestions, sources of supplies, mail zip codes, motel and campground locations, emergency phone numbers, precautions, landowner restrictions, and natural or historic items of interest are given for each trail.

The trail data is listed in north-to-south (or east-to-west) and in the reverse direction so that the same page and map can be used for hiking in either direction. For loop trails, miles are listed in clockwise or counterclockwise direction. Key data points are numbered both on the data page and on the map so the hiker can relate written data to map features. The map shows the trail location in a dashed line on a base map. The mileage scale is shown as "1 section = 1 square mile." This section is the land area marked off by squares numbered from 1 to 36. Since the sides of these squares measure one mile they provide a ready mileage scale anywhere on the map. The counties involved are listed on the map page.

Call the FTA (1-800-343-1882, in Florida) for additional information about trail sections.

Reading a Map Title Block

> **JONES SWAMP**
> **State Monument**
> **FLORIDA TRAIL**
> **18.6 MILES**
> Scale: 1 section = 1 Square Mile

Title blocks in this book give the name and any governmental designations involving the area. Below the main title is the total mileage of the trail, including all cross and side trails. Below that is the scale statement.

Reading a Data Page

Mileage S to N		Mileage N to S
13.0	Terminus at State Monument entrance.	0.0
10.5 ①	**Junction** with **woods road.**	2.5
9.0	Route **turns** at creek overlook.	4.0
8.0	Trail **follows** old tramway for 3.0 miles.	5.0
3.5	**Leave/arrive** woods near county park.	9.5
0.0	Terminus near gate to county park.	13.0

Above is a sample listing of some of the types of entries included on data pages in this book. The circled number at the left indicates a data point on the map described by that line of data. The word "junction" is used to describe the coming together of the trail and some other path. That other "path" may be a side trail, dike, woods road or graded road. Woods roads are a loose term for a detectable two track path that vehicles use, or had used infrequently. These paths are usually grassy and overgrown.

The word "turns" is used to describe an abrupt change in the direction of the trail. A double blaze alerts the hiker to a turn; a single blaze should be visible on the trail in the new direction.

The term "leave/arrive" is a bi-directional way of stating that the trail is close to some change point.

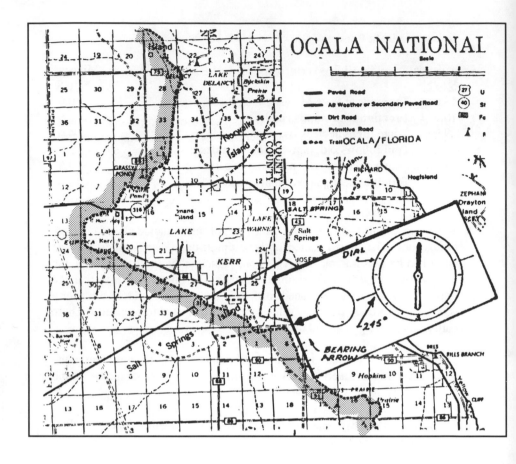

Using Map and Compass

1. Place the compass on or near the map with the bearing arrow pointing in the direction of travel.
2. Rotate the map to line up the north arrow on the map north with the compass needle.
3. Turn the rotating dial on the compass to bring its N over the red end of the compass needle.
4. Read the bearing on the compass dial.
5. Holding the compass with the needle under N, sight along the bearing arrow and choose a landmark to walk toward.

TIPS FOR HIKERS

Trail Instructions and Restrictions

Trail Marking
Carry and study the trail maps when hiking, and use a compass. There will
be a FT sign post at most trailheads. Mapped sections of the trail are marked
with painted blazes. The primary trail is marked with orange blazes, except in
state parks where the blazes are white. Blue blazes mark side trails to
campsites, access points or places of interest. Double blazes indicate a change
of direction, or that the trail is leaving an obvious path. After you spot a double
blaze, watch carefully for the next blaze. If you go more than a few steps
without seeing a blaze, you may have lost the trail. Stop and retrace your steps.
If blazes have been obliterated or have faded, please make a note and report
them to the FTA office. Trail relocations are made frequently. *Always give the
blazes priority over the map.*

Parking Along the Trail
Park in recommended sites when possible. Vandalism may occur. Do not
leave valuables in a car.

Registers
Register boxes are stationed at points along the trail. Be sure to sign in
when you hike. The registers provide a valuable record of trail use and are
of special importance to rescue personnel.

The Compass
Carry a compass and map when you hike in unfamiliar territory. You will
need them to find the trail again if blazes have been destroyed by fire or
clear-cuts.

Using map and compass is called "orienteering" and is a fascinating sport in
itself. A compass and map are useful to find some scenic place near the trail
and then return, or to get back quickly to the trailhead in an emergency. In most
places getting lost is merely an aggravating waste of time, but on a few sections
of the trail, such as the Bradwell Bay "Titi Wilderness," a hiker can get into
serious trouble without a compass and map.

Trash
Don't pollute the forest. Pack out what you bring in and bring extra plastic
bags for trash. Make sure trash bags are well sealed, because food odors will
attract animals. Pick up egg shells, orange peels and food scraps when you
wash dishes. Use sand or a pine cone as an abrasive to scrub pans.

1

Pets
Pets are allowed in Florida's state parks in daytime on a leash. They are not permitted in campgrounds at night. Other hikers do not know your dog as well as you do. In fairness to them and to wildlife in the area, keep your dog restrained while you hike the trail.

Guns
Guns should not be carried on the trail when hiking.

Wildlife Management Area Permits
Permits may be required when using some sections of the trail. They can be obtained at any county courthouse or county tax agent office for a moderate cost.

Trail Tips

Notes for Beginning Hikers
Perhaps you are interested in hiking in Florida but are reluctant to try because of fear of the wilderness, or because you worry that you are not physically capable. Hiking the Florida Trail should not be frightening or strenuous, though, and new hikers have much to look forward to. Backpackers enjoy solitude and natural scenery. If you walk quietly, early in the day and in small groups, you will see more wildlife.

Florida Trail hikers range in age from young children to senior citizens. The trail offers many kinds of hiking for all kinds of people. If you are worried about your physical endurance or your children's attention spans, you can plan short, leisurely hikes at first, but don't underestimate yourself: FTA has members who are grandparents and are vigorous, experienced hikers. Some of them maintain their own sections of the trail. Use good judgement, and if you have medical problems, talk to your doctor before embarking on a strenuous hike.

First Aid and Emergency Supplies to Take on *Every* Hike
Pack a bag of emergency supplies and keep it with your hiking day pack:

Band-aids	whistle	insect repellant
gauze pads	aspirin	matches or lighter
bandana	burn cream	sunscreen
flashlight	safety pins	moleskin
knife	compass	cup
quarter (phone)	pen, paper	canteen or water bottle
name, address, phone of emergency contact		

Clothing

Shorts and a T-shirt are adequate for many Florida day hikes. A day-pack to hold a sweater and a poncho, your first aid kit, food, water, camera and perhaps dry socks will cover warm weather hiking. Long pants and long sleeves protect you from insects and brush. If you are backpacking, learn to travel light. After four miles, a loaded pack seems to double in weight.

Shoes

FT hikers wear everything from tennis shoes to expensive hiking boots. Jogging shoes or inexpensive work boots are also popular. Compared to the mountains, Florida terrain is forgiving. If you are carrying a heavy pack, be sure your shoes provide good arch support.

Toilet

Move at least 30 yards off the trail and dig a hole with boot or trowel about six inches deep, six inches wide and a foot long. Cover with the excavated dirt. Pack out all toilet paper or towelettes.

Shelter

Shelter is not necessary for survival on the Florida Trail, but because winter temperatures can drop into the twenties or lower in Central or North Florida, a tent is desirable. An inexpensive pup tent is adequate under most circumstances. Other tents offer more space, less weight, better water protection and other advantages. Backpackers may prefer an ultra light weight tent. Check with an experienced hiker or ask at a trail shop before buying an expensive tent.

A lightweight sleeping bag is fine for Florida. Synthetic filler dries fast and should provide insulation even when wet. Down gives much warmth for little weight and can be compressed. Backpackers may be willing to pay the extra cost for a down bag. Many FT hikers carry a hip-to-shoulder foam pad about 3/4 to 1 1/2 inches thick to make sleeping more comfortable.

Camp Fires

Open fires pose a real threat to the woods during dry weather. Fires are forbidden during drought. Don't build a fire for cooking unless you are certain that open fires are permitted. Build the fire on bare ground, and after it burns out, eliminate all traces of the fire ring. Try to erase all signs of your campsite so that the next hiker will find an unspoiled spot.

Stoves

Anyone who plans to become a backpacker should obtain a small lightweight stove. These range from inexpensive and inefficient alcohol paste stoves to intricate, expensive gasoline or propane stoves. *Don't use a stove in a tent.* Besides the danger of fire, stoves produce carbon monoxide which can be fatal inside a closed tent.

Water
Do not drink stream or surface water without filtering, chemically treating or boiling it. Even a crystal clear stream deep in the woods may be contaminated. *The giardiasis parasite is prevalent in untreated water* and can cause severe stomach upsets including diarrhea and cramps from one to three weeks after exposure. Boiling water for 3 to 5 minutes should kill the parasites. Water from wells designated as potable on the maps is safe to drink. Water may be hidden in advance at strategic crossroads. A collapsible water carrier is handy to transport a gallon back to camp from a nearby water source.

Whatever the arrangements, plan to use at least three quarts of water per day. In very hot weather, it is wise to carry a mineral replenishing powdered drink mix to add to the water.

Food
Carry enough food to replace the calories used while hiking. Eat small amounts at frequent rest stops and the largest meal in the evening. You can purchase trail food (fruit, granola, etc.) and food for meals anywhere; it is not necessary to buy it at a trail shop. Candy and dried fruit give energy.

A light breakfast is advisable, perhaps an instant cereal with fruit and beverage. Canned or freeze-dried dinners are simple to prepare for supper and tasty concoctions can be made from dried noodle or soup mixes. Experienced hikers will have interesting recipes to share with a beginner.

Organizing a Pack for an Overnight
Backpacks usually have one or two large compartments and several smaller pockets. Pack so that the heaviest gear (tent, food, stove) is nearest your back and hips, and the things you need often (map, compass, rainwear) are easy to reach in a hurry. A sleeping bag can be rolled and tied below your pack. Distribute the weight so you can walk without leaning far forward.

Backpacking gear needn't be expensive. Check your kitchen for light-weight containers. Half-gallon juice jugs are good water bottles. Film cannisters or plastic spice jars can hold small items.

Reduce weight wherever possible: repackage food in plastic bags and carry dehydrated food when you can. Take only what you think you will need and revise your list after each trip.

Suggested Supply Checklist for an Overnight

Kitchen

two quarts of water, minimum
stove and fuel, aluminum foil
knife, spoon, can opener
matches
water treatment tablets/ filter

paper towels
trash bag
cooking pot, pot lifter
condiments
cup, bowl or plate

Shelter

tent and ground cloth
sleeping bag/foam pad

plastic to sit on

Clothing

boots and camp shoes
two pairs of socks
raingear, poncho, hat
T - shirt, underwear
long-sleeved shirt
jeans or shorts
jacket or windbreaker

Personal

toilet paper, plastic trowel
medicine
comb, brush
toothbrush, paste
soap and towel
moleskin

Miscellaneous

map and compass
lighter, matches
camera, binoculars

first aid kit & insect repellant
flashlight
nylon cord

The Loaded Backpack

Flap Pocket

maps
notebook
pen

Top Side Pockets
canteen
stove, fuel
raingear
lunch

Top Compartment
cup
spoon
jacket
raingear
plastic bags

Lower Side Pockets
first aid kit
sun screen
insect repellant
flashlight
toilet kit
matches

Bottom Compartment
stove
tent
cook kit
clothes
food

Stuff Bag
sleeping bag
foam pad

Problems and Precautions

This section of the guide should help hikers understand potential problems and the precautions to take to prevent them. If you plan to do extended hiking or to make it a serious hobby, read one of the many books about wilderness survival. (Colin Fletcher's *Complete Walker* series is fun to read.)

Snakes
The possibility of snakebite on the trail is very low. It can be reduced further by a few simple precautions:
* Stay on the trail when possible.
* Don't put your hands or feet into holes.
* When stepping over a large rock or log, look first for a snake on the blind side.
* Be careful around piles of brush or rocks.
* Don't walk at night before your eyes are accustomed to the dark (use a flashlight).
* Don't handle crippled, sluggish or "dead" snakes.

Learn which Florida snakes are poisonous; most are not. The best way to combat poisonous snakebite is to keep the victim still and calm and find a doctor quickly. Attempts to "suck out the poison" do more harm than good, and cheap snakebite kits are not effective. Snakebite is sometimes very painful, but most victims survive.

Alligators
Alligators seldom bother people and when they do, it is usually a result of people's ignorant or aggressive behavior. Leave alligators alone; don't bother their eggs or young, and don't deliberately cut off an alligator's escape route to the water. If you swim in unknown waters, you run the risk of an alligator encounter. *Do not feed alligators*.

Other Animals
Feeding wild animals is dangerous because the animals learn to regard humans as a food source and subsequently become unnaturally "friendly." Sometimes it's extremely tempting. A wild animal may seem to be begging you for a potato chip, but you must resist.

Aside from poisonous snakes and alligators, there are no dangerous wild animals in Florida. Bobcats and bears don't attack people unless they are deliberately threatened or cornered. Never touch a wild animal. Their ticks and fleas might carry disease. More importantly, wild animals may be rabid. Keep your distance from animals who are unusually weak, act strange or seem aggressive. If you meet animals whose behavior is odd or offensive, report them to the nearest Sheriff's office or to the Florida Game and Fresh Water Fish Commission's nearest agent. *Don't feed any wild animals.*

Getting Lost
Always carry a compass and a trail map. If you do not have a map, find someone who has one and keep him/her in sight. Tell someone where you are going before you leave and when you plan to return.

If you are lost, stay in one spot and don't wander. Carry a whistle or mirror to signal search and rescue personnel. Three toots of a whistle or flashes of a mirror are universal signals for help. If you are lost for several hours, you may feel inclined to panic, but do not. Sit down and assess the situation. If you leave the cleared trail, it will be difficult to travel in brush, palmetto, or vine-tangled wilderness without getting exhausted and more lost.

Night
The first night in the woods in a tent can be scary to a novice hiker. Sounds are greatly magnified and there are many strange noises. An armadillo sniffing and moving through dry palmetto leaves conjures up visions of a wild beast looking for prey, but armadillos don't eat people, and neither does anything else in Florida; you are safe in your tent.

Walking at night is fun, but you may want to wait until your night vision is good (about 20 minutes). Stars in the wilderness far from cities are beautifully bright, and moonlight reflecting off the sandy paths shows the way.

Insect Bites
A hiker is far more likely to be bitten by an insect than by a snake. This is the experience of FTA members when on work hikes where there is a lot of cutting, chopping, and disturbing of the vegetation. Everyone is familiar with mosquitoes, and they may be severe in south Florida. Other insects to expect are:

Chiggers: Chiggers (red bugs) are tiny brown bugs that get through openings in clothing at the ankles, wrists and waist, burrow into your skin and cause you to itch. Insect repellent, especially if it contains *DEET* (diethyltoluamide), will help to keep them off. You can also use a mixture of talc and powdered sulfur (ask your pharmacist) on your ankles. The sulfur mixture will also keep ticks at bay. A folded poncho or square of plastic to sit on will help deter insects.

Ticks: Be concerned about ticks. Certain species of them carry Lyme disease, which can be seriously debilitating if not treated promptly. The Florida Department of Agriculture and Consumer Services, Division of Forestry suggests the following preventative steps:
*   Wear long pants and a long-sleeved shirt.
*   Tuck in shirt tails and pull socks up over pant cuffs.
*   While outside, check clothes for ticks. When you come home, inspect yourself thoroughly; pay special attention to groin, back, armpits and head.

If you find a tick on your body, follow these steps:
*   Gently tug on the head of the tick with tweezers at the place where it is attached to the skin. Do not crush the body or leave any of the mouth parts in the skin. The barbed mouth parts do not release easily, so be patient.
*   Wipe the bite with an antiseptic.
*   At home, save the tick in a jar with a moistened cotton ball and refrigerate. If a rash or other symptoms develop, take the tick to your physician. Otherwise, you can discard it.

Early symptoms of Lyme disease are usually flu-like: fever, muscle aches, fatigue. If left untreated, the disease may cause swollen joints, headaches, meningitis, facial paralysis, dizziness, irregular heartbeat and fainting.

Bees, Wasps and Hornets: A hiker with a history of severe reactions to bee or wasp stings (prolonged severe swelling, stiffness, and pain or shock) should not go on extended hikes without a prescription sting kit. People who experience painful swelling may get some relief from the over-the-counter antihistamines and   pain-relieving ointments sold at drug stores.

Caterpillars, Ants and Other Insects: Some of these insects can give a painful sting, but they are seldom more than a nuisance. If a serious reaction does occur, medical attention may be necessary. If the reaction is allergic, an antihistamine may help, but be sure to use only the prescribed dose.

Poisonous Plants
Poison ivy, oak and sumac, found in Florida, can cause an irritating rash. Many other shrubs, such as Brazilian pepper and oleander, can produce allergic reactions in susceptible people.

Lightning
Florida is the lightning capital of the United States. Be wary of lightning and minimize the risks of being struck while outdoors. If an electrical storm approaches:

* Stay away from isolated tall trees.
* Don't be the tallest object in the immediate area.
* If you're in the open, crouch with your hands on your shoes.
* If you're carrying a pack with an aluminum frame, take it off and move some distance away from it.

Infection

Cuts and scratches should be treated promptly with disinfectant and kept clean. Infections can occur if a small wound is contaminated by polluted water, soil or rotting vegetation. Be sure your tetanus shots are up to date.

Heat Exhaustion

Heat exhaustion can be very serious, but can easily be avoided. Symptoms include irregular pulse, pallor, nausea, weakness. and heavy sweating. To avoid heat exhaustion, rest frequently, drink more water than thirst requires, and eat salty snacks or drink a mineral replenishing drink. On group hikes, don't worry about annoying other hikers by asking to slow down or take a rest stop. Hikers with heart problems should be cautious about hot weather exertion and should consult a physician before hiking.

Hypothermia

Hypothermia is a potentially dangerous response to chilling. Most deaths from exposure are due to hypothermia, which *can* occur above the freezing point. In fact, most cases of hypothermia develop in air temperatures between 30 and 50 degrees Fahrenheit. Symptoms are uncontrollable shivering, clumsiness and confusion. Simple precautions eliminate the danger of hypothermia. The key is to keep the body core (trunk) from getting chilled. Head covering is important; much body heat is lost through the head. Wear layers of clothing which can be removed as needed. This will prevent clothes from getting wet from perspiration. Drink lots of water and eat energy-producing snacks frequently.

If you get wet, try to save body core heat. Keep a plastic vapor barrier (plastic trash bags, for instance) around the wet clothes. Stripping off wet clothes immediately may severely chill the body and rubbing hands and feet will draw heat from the body. Start a camp stove, heat up something sweet to drink, and set up some type of shelter. After a warm drink and high energy snack, change into dry clothes. If chilling seems severe, get into a dry sleeping bag.

Victims of severe hypothermia become disoriented and may behave irrationally, perhaps doing themselves further harm or refusing help. It is imperative that anyone in this condition be made warm quickly, even if physical restraint must be used. Hypothermia can be fatal.

10

FLORIDA BIOLOGICAL COMMUNITIES

Swamp Forests

Deciduous hardwood swamps are found along rivers and in basins where the forest floor is saturated or submerged part of the year. Other terms for this community are floodplain forest, hydric hammock and river swamp.

Plants: This community is characterized by large hardwoods such as blackgum, water tupelo, pop ash, red maple, sweetgum, water oak and water hickory. Other typical overstory trees are bald cypress and cabbage palm. Understory trees include buttonbush, dahoon, wax-myrtle, American hornbeam and elderberry. Most plants in mixed hardwood swamps are deciduous. Swamp forest productivity and species mixtures are determined to a large degree by the kind and condition of alluvial soil deposits.

Animals: River swamps provide habitat for a wide variety of animals, some of them rare species. If the ivory-billed woodpecker still exists in this state, as some ornithologists suspect, it probably inhabits large swamp forests. Other swamp animals are the bobcat, deer, turkey, gray squirrel, otter, pileated woodpecker, wood duck, and numerous songbirds, turtles and snakes.

Cypress Swamps

Cypress swamps are usually located along rivers or lakes or scattered through other communities such as flatwoods or dry prairies. They also occur along shallow drainage systems known as sloughs or strands. Cypress swamps have water at or above ground level for much of the year.

Plants: The bald-cypress is the dominant tree along lakes and streams. The pond cypress occurs in cypress heads and domes, which are typically interspersed through flatwoods and prairies. Trees often found with cypress include blackgum, red maple, willow, pop ash, pond pine and slash pine. The overall tree diversity of cypress heads is relatively low, that of strands and stream margin forests is somewhat higher. Smaller plants include wax-myrtle, buttonbush, various ferns, poison ivy, greenbrier and numerous air plants. Arrowhead, pickerelweed, sawgrass, and other marsh plants are often found in areas of open water within cypress swamps.

Animals: The deeper cypress swamps have rather limited populations of wildlife but aquatic animals such as salamanders, water snakes, alligators and otters may be abundant. More shallow, seasonally flooded areas such as cypress heads are refuge areas for deer and other large animals.

11

Dry Prairies

Dry prairies are vast, treeless plains. They often form an intermediate community between wet, grassy areas and upland forests. The largest areas of dry prairie occur north and west of Lake Okeechobee.

Plants: Dry prairies are dominated by grasses including wiregrass, broom sedges and several different carpet grasses. Saw palmetto is the most common shrub, and fetterbush, staggerbush and blueberry are also common. Many sedges and herbs grow in the dry prairie. Scattered throughout are small bayheads, cypress domes and cabbage palm-live oak hammocks.

Animals: Dry prairies often have large wildlife populations. Characteristic birds include the caracara, sandhill crane, meadowlark and burrowing owl. The cotton rat, bobcat and raccoon are common.

Scrub Cypress

Scrub cypress areas are found on frequently flooded rock and marl soils in South Florida. The largest areas of scrub cypress occur in eastern Collier County and northern Monroe County.

Plants: Scrub cypress forests resemble marshes with dwarfed pond cypress scattered throughout. Much of the vegetation is similar, including scattered sawgrass, beakrushes, St. John's wort and wax-myrtle. Air plants grow on the cypress trees, and there are occasional orchids.

Animals: The poor soil and lack of nutrients that are responsible for the sparse vegetation also account for a fairly scattered wildlife population. Wood storks, occasional roseate spoonbills and alligators may be encountered, along with deer and bobcats.

Pine Flatwoods

Flatwoods are the most abundant community in Florida. Before 1900 they covered half the state. Most flatwoods occur on the level areas, or terraces, between ancient shorelines. Layers of marine sand accumulated on these terraces in prehistoric times, when they were covered by shallow seas.

Longleaf pine flatwoods are found on better drained sites. Slash pine flatwoods are usually found in areas of intermediate wetness. Pond pines predominate in the wettest areas.

Plants: Flatwoods have few tree species. Shrubs and small trees vary among the three major types, but many plants are common to all flatwoods communities. Common understory plants include wiregrass, saw palmetto, wax-myrtle, gallberry and fetterbush. Flatwoods are usually sprinkled with cypress domes, bayheads or small titi swamps.

Animals: Flatwoods have a fairly large and diverse animal population. The larger animals, such as deer, bears, bobcats, raccoons, and gray foxes, are most commonly found around the boundaries between the flatwoods and hammocks, cypress heads, bayheads, titi swamps and open areas. Other animals of the flatwoods include fox squirrels, cotton rats, black snakes and cottontails. Birds include the brown-headed nuthatch, the Bachman's warbler, and the rufous-sided towhee.

Hammocks
Hammock is a Florida term for a cluster of broad-leaved trees. Trees in hammocks are often evergreen and usually grow in relatively rich soil. The hammock community is similar in many respects to the mixed hardwood and pine of the panhandle. It is the climax vegetation of most areas of central and peninsular Florida; the mixed hardwood and pine community is the climax community of the panhandle area. Central Florida hammocks occur on fairly rich sandy soils rather than the clay of the panhandle community and are prevalent in areas where limestone is near the surface. Hammocks can be further classified on the basis of vegetation into upland hammocks, coastal hammocks, and live oak-cabbage palm hammocks, which are scattered within other communities. Hammocks are similar to the mixed hardwood and pine woods of the panhandle but lack the shortleaf pine, American beech and other more northern vegetation.

Plants: Characteristic trees of central Florida hammocks are southern magnolia, laurel oak and American holly. Live oak-cabbage palm hammocks are dominated by those two species.

Animals: Hammock animals include the spadefoot toad, tufted titmouse, great crested flycatcher, golden mouse, wood rat and flying squirrel.

Tropical Hammocks
Tropical and semi-tropical hammocks are found on many of the tree islands in the Everglades. Remnants of semi-tropical hammocks occur north to Palm Beach on the east coast and Sarasota on the west coast.

Plants: Tropical hammocks typically have very high plant diversity, containing over thirty-five species of trees and almost sixty-five species of shrubs and small trees. Typical tropical trees are the strangler fig, gumbo-limbo, mastic, bustic, lancewood, the ironwoods, poisonwood, pigeon plum and Jamaica dogwood. Vines, air plants and ferns are often abundant.

Animals: Tropical hammocks are extremely important to several species of wildlife in southern Florida, including the cotton mouse, woodrat, grey squirrel and marsh rabbit.

Mixed Hardwood and Pine
The mixed hardwood and pine community is the southern-most extension of the southern Piedmont mixed hardwood forest. It occurs on the clay soils of the northern panhandle.

Plants: Younger growth may be primarily pine with shortleaf and loblolly pines predominant, but as succession continues various hardwoods become dominant. Hardwood trees of this area include American beech, Southern magnolia, Florida maple and numerous others. The understory includes dogwood, red mulberry, hop-hornbeam, American hornbeam and redbud.

Animals: The types of animal vary with the maturity of the forest. Rapidly reproducing, broadly adapted species such as cottontails and bobwhites are typical early succession animals; more narrowly adapted species such as woodpeckers, moles and woodcock are typical of more mature forests. Other characteristic animals include the barred owl, pileated woodpecker, red-bellied woodpecker, white-tailed deer, gray squirrel, shrews, gray fox and cotton mouse.

Sandhill Community
Sandhill communities occur on well-drained, deep and relatively sterile sands.

Plants: Because of the harsh conditions (poor soil, low moisture and fire) this community has a low tree diversity. Longleaf pines form a scattered (thirty to one hundred trees per acre) overstory in mature natural stands. Often today, oaks such as turkey oak and southern red oak form the overstory, with the pines logged out and periodic fires eliminated. In natural stands the oaks form a relatively open understory, and plants such as wiregrass and yellow foxglove provide fairly complete ground cover.

Animals: Many of the animals found in this community are burrowers, an adaptation to high temperatures and dry conditions. Indigo snakes, gopher tortoises, fence lizards, ground doves, bobwhites, rufous-sided towhees, fox squirrels and pocket gophers are typical vertebrates of the sandhill community. The rare red-cockaded woodpecker inhabits old trees in mature sandhill communities.

Ecology: Fire is the dominant factor in the ecology of sandhill communities. The interrelationships of the sandhill vegetation, particularly the longleaf pine-wiregrass relationship, are dependent on frequent (every two to five years) ground fires. Longleaf pine is sensitive to hardwood competition. Wiregrass helps to prevent the germination of hardwood seeds and ensures that there is sufficient fuel buildup on the floor of the community to carry a fire over large areas.

Sand Pine Scrub
Sand pine scrub forests grow on ancient sand dunes far inland from the present coast. The Ocala National Forest's Big Scrub is 35 miles long by 15 miles wide, and is the largest sand pine scrub forest anywhere.

Plants: Sand pine scrub is typically two-layered, with sand pine occupying the top layer and various oaks and other shrubs making up a thick understory. Ground cover is sparse or absent, and large areas of white to gray sand normally occur throughout. Understory plants include myrtle oak, sand-live oak, Chapman's oak, rosemary and gopher-apple. Except for a tiny area of sand pine scrub in southeast Alabama, this plant community is found only in Florida.

Animals: Most of the animals are adapted to high temperatures and a scarcity of water. Typical animals include the gopher frog, scrub lizard, sand skink, black racer, Florida mouse and scrub jay.

Ecology: The sand pine scrub is essentially a fire-based community. Its fire regime, however, differs greatly from those of the flatwoods and sandhills terrain. Ground cover is sparse and leaf fall is minimal, thus reducing the chance of the frequent ground fires so important in the sand hill community. As the sand pines mature, however, they retain most of their branches, building up large fuel supplies in the crowns. The thick understory vegetation and these retained branches provide ready pathways to the highly combustible crown. When a fire does occur (every twenty to forty years) this fuel supply, in combination with the sand pine's relatively low resistance to fire and the high stand density, assure a hot, fast burning fire. In 1935, one such fire consumed 35,000 acres of scrub in four hours.

Fire allows for regeneration of the sand pine community, which would otherwise pass into a xeric hammock. Regeneration usually results in evenly aged stands of trees. The Ocala variety of sand pine (dominant in the peninsula) is so adapted to fire regeneration that intense heat is needed to open its cones.

15

Salt Marshes

Salt marshes occur on low wave-energy shorelines north of the range of the mangroves and among the mangroves in many areas of south Florida. Salt marshes also extend up into tidal rivers.

Plants: Many salt marshes are dominated by one plant, usually cordgrass or black rush. The species existing in any one area usually depend on the degree of inundation by tides and the salinity of the water. Salt marshes often blend gradually with freshwater marshes, forming a transition zone of saltwater and freshwater plants.

Animals: Salt marshes harbor large numbers of invertebrates which are fed upon by many of the higher animals of the marsh and estuary. Birds are particularly numerous in and around salt marshes. Rails, egrets, gulls, terns and seaside sparrows depend on the marsh for food. The diamond-back terrapin, salt marsh snake, mink, otter and raccoon are other characteristic animals.

Freshwater Marshes and Wet Prairies

Freshwater marshes are grass-sedge-rush communities occurring in areas where the soil is usually saturated or covered with surface water for two or more months during the year. Wet prairies are characterized by less water and more grasses than marshes and usually have fewer of the tall emergents such as bulrushes. This category also includes the wet to dry marshes and prairies found on marl areas in south Florida.

Plants: More than 15 different types of marshes and wet prairies have been identified in Florida. These include sawgrass marshes; flag marshes dominated by pickerelweed, arrowhead, fire flag and other non-grass herbs; cattail marshes; spike-rush marshes; bulrush marshes; maidencane prairies; grass, rush and sedge prairies and switch grass prairies dominated by taller grasses. Any single marsh may have different sections composed of these major types, and there is almost complete intergradation between the types.

Animals: Many rare and endangered species depend heavily on this habitat; the everglades kite, wood stork, Cape Sable seaside sparrow, sandhill crane, alligator, Florida round-tailed muskrat, and Everglades mink all are found in this habitat. So, too, are many wading birds and waterfowl (wintering and resident), numerous frogs and other amphibians, various turtles and otters.

16

SOUTH FLORIDA

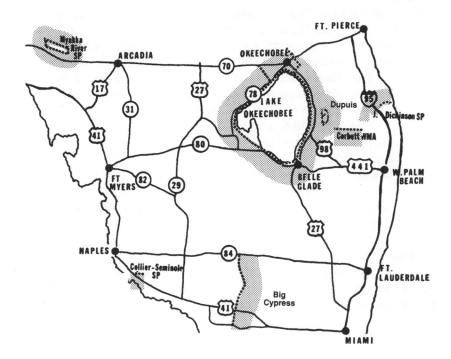

The trails in this area include those in Big Cypress National Preserve near Everglades National Park, the dikes around Lake Okeechobee, trails in three state parks and on South Florida Water Management District land.

The trails in the southernmost section of south Florida pass through a combination of cypress swamp and sawgrass marsh interspersed with tropical hammocks. In the north part, the trails pass near the huge dike around Lake Okeechobee and the southern end of the Kissimmee River. This Everglades region is unique and the hiking experience here is rugged but well worth the effort. Frequent wading should be expected, except on dikes. Myakka River State Park has over 45 miles of excellent trail into remote areas of the park. Collier-Seminole State Park has probably the only true tropical trail in the country. The trail atop the Herbert Hoover Dike around Lake Okeechobee on the west side is shaded with beautiful views of the lake. The east side offers almost continuous views of the lakeshore ecology with long, shadeless exposure. Hikers can watch birds, fish and, on the east side, step off the trail to take a cool dip in the lake.

Big Cypress National Preserve

Location
The trail is in the Big Cypress National Preserve, which is managed by the National Park Service. The northern terminus is at the preserve boundary, six miles south of SR 84 (Alligator Alley). The southern terminus is on SR 94 (Loop Road), 15 miles west of the Baptist church at the forty mile bend of US 41. Part of Loop Road is unimproved dirt, and caution is advised. Travel for the last seven miles will be slow. Access is available on Tamiami Trail (US 41) at Oasis Ranger Station, 55 miles west of the Dade County courthouse, 42 miles west of the Florida Turnpike, and 52 miles east of Naples. From this location, head north, or south to Loop Road.

Type of Hiking
Wading should be expected during average years in the northern third of the area below Alligator Alley and normally in the Loop Road section. January through April are the drier months.

Parking
On US 41, parking is available at the National Park Service Building, Oasis Ranger Station. Park on the east or west side of the building. Check in at Oasis Ranger Station before leaving your vehicle. Do not block any gates or the front entrance.

Water
There is water at Oasis Ranger Station and in wells at campsites north of US 41. Treat all well or ground water; there should be containers of water at the wells so that you can prime the pumps. Make sure you refill these containers for the next users.

Conveniences
Supplies: On US 41 at Monroe Station 5 miles west of Oasis.
Mail: Ochopee 33943
Motels: Everglades City
Public Campgrounds: Big Cypress National Preserve, at Midway Lake, and at Monument Lake. No facilities at either campground. Collier-Seminole State Park on US 41 near SR92.

Emergency
Collier County Sheriff: 305-547-7498
National Park Service: 813-695-4111/4112 and 305-247-6211 (24 hours)

Precautions
Carry extra shoes and socks. Always carry a map and compass in this remote section. In high water footing can be tricky. Watch for pinnacle rock and ruts. For Preserve information, write to Star Route, Box 110, Ochopee, FL 33943. Phone: 813-695-2000.

Restrictions
The trail north of the Big Cypress National Preserve boundary is on private property. Hikers must be members of the FTA to use this portion.

Description
This trail passes through the great swamp of dwarf pond cypress and alternates with pine islands, hammocks, giant ferns, and prairies with cabbage palm and saw palmetto. Bromeliads (air plants) are everywhere. The Seven Mile Camp is a particularly interesting wildlife location, where the night sounds of the chuck-will's-widows mingle with the occasional screams of a bobcat or the sound of wild turkeys. Bluebirds, quail, kites, wood storks, short-tailed hawks and the endangered red-cockaded woodpecker can also be seen. Big Cypress is also home to eagles, deer, alligators, bear, feral hogs and Florida panthers. Alligator holes can sometimes be detected in drier weather when water level is down. Big Cypress National Preserve consists of 900 square miles of subtropical terrain, about a third of which is covered with the dwarf pond cypress. Bordering on the north edge of Everglades National Park, it is named for its great expanse, not the size of the trees. The land is not totally a swamp because it is laced with sandy islands of slash pine and hardwood hammocks. There are sloughs, wet prairies, marshes and mangrove forests as well.

Trail Data - Big Cypress

Mileage S to N		Mileage N to S
31.0 ③	Public part of the trail stops at the boundary of Big Cypress National Preserve.	0.0
29.0	Trail follows road.	2.0
28.1	Do not cross fence.	2.9
25.0	Pass campsite, well in cabbage palm area.	6.0
22.3	Blue-blazed loop trail (point D) joins from north.	8.7
18.1	Cross road and pass campsite, well.	12.9
15.2	Blue-blazed loop trail (point B) joins from west.	15.8
15.1	Pass campsite, well in pine and palmetto area at "Seven-Mile Camp."	15.9
11.2	Blue-blazed loop trail (point A) joins from west.	19.8
8.6	Pass Florida Trail sign.	22.4
8.3 ②	Trail crosses US 41 (Tamiami Trail) at National Park Service building (Oasis Ranger Station). Parking, water, register. Zero degree north/180 degree south compass course ends/begins at FT signpost 200 yards southeast from phone booth.	22.7
7.4	Cross swamp buggy trail. Large blaze shows 0/180 heading. Maintain 0/180 course crossing old swamp buggy roads several times in area of cypress heads and cypress prairie.	23.6
5.8	Leave from/arrive at old east-west tramway in Roberts Lake Strand. May be under water in wet year. Blazes start/stop here. Campsite (no well) at abandoned cabin on dry ground on end of tramway.	25.2
3.0	Pass campsite, well in high and dry hammock on edge of prairie. May be under water in wet year. Follow Sawmill Road for 3.0 miles through pine and cypress areas.	28.0
0.0 ①	South terminus of Florida Trail at loop road (SR 94)-Sawmill Road intersection.	31.0

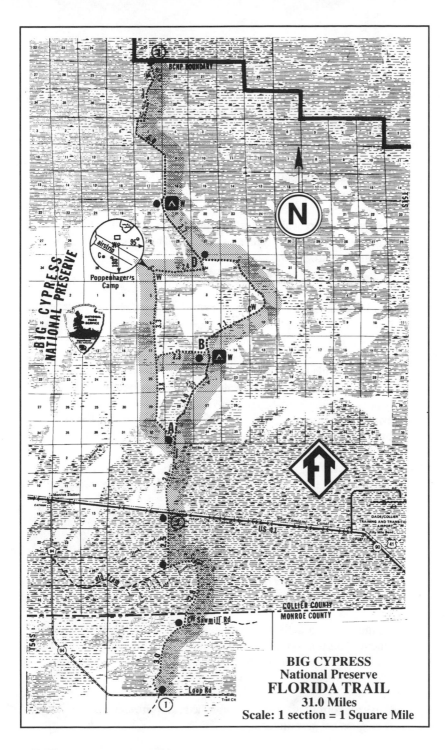

BIG CYPRESS
National Preserve
FLORIDA TRAIL
31.0 Miles
Scale: 1 section = 1 Square Mile

Collier, Monroe Counties

Collier - Seminole State Park

Location
The entrance to the park is 17 miles southeast of Naples on US 41, Tamiami Trail, on the south side of the highway, 0.25 mile southeast of the SR 92-US 41 intersection. Reach the trail terminus via the park service road on the north side of US 41, 0.7 mile southeast of the park entrance. The terminus is 0.25 mile north on the east side of the park service road.

Type of Hiking
There is mixed wet and dry walking through this, the most tropical trail in the country, an example of true Everglades environment. This park has Royal Palm trees growing in the wild.

Parking
Park at the hiker's parking area on the west side of the park service road near the trail terminus.

Water
Potable water is available at the park. There is no water at the campsite. Treat all ground water. Carry four quarts of water for each overnight backpacker.

Conveniences
Supplies: General store, gas, restaurant at SR 92-US 41 intersection.
Mail: Marco 33937
Motels: Naples, Marco
Public Campground: In the park on south side of US 41. Heavily used during winter season.

Emergency
Park Manager 813-394-3446
Collier County Sheriff: 813-774-4434
Park Office (day): 813-394-3397

Precautions
Backpackers must register at the park office. Bears roam the park. Hang food away from them. This trail is blazed white, with side trails blazed in blue. Do not approach the Indian settlement from the trail.

Restrictions
No ground fires are permitted. Use the established campfire spot. No vehicles, horses, pets or guns are permitted.

Description

The park is located where the lush tropical forest meets the Big Cypress swamp environment. The south side of the park is mostly mangrove, salt marsh, and estuary. The hiking trail on the north side of US 41 winds through tropical hammock. Miccosukee Indians have a settlement close to the Florida trail; stay on the trail when passing it. One of the largest native Royal Palms anywhere grows along the trail. The campsite is in a high, dry oak hammock. The western part of the trail is wet in most seasons, and the rest of the trail is varied, much of it dry. Strangler fig can be found wild in the forest. Exotic trees and shrubs, such as Brazilian pepper and melaleuca, have found footing here and are prolific. The animals found here include the Florida black bear.

Trail Data - Collier - Seminole State Park

Mileage Clockwise			Mileage Counterclockwise
		Access to main loop trail via 0.1 mile blue-blazed trail near the parking area. Look for sign.	
6.1	①	Junction of main loop with access trail.	0.0
4.7		Cross park service road.	1.4
4.5		Cross park service road.	1.6
3.5		Junction of main loop with 0.4 mile blue-blazed trail to campsite in beautiful tropical hammock. No water.	2.6
1.8		Trail passes through wetter section of the loop.	4.3
1.0		Pass near Indian village. Don't approach from trail.	5.1
0.1		Cross park service road.	6.0
0.0		Junction of main loop with access trail.	6.1

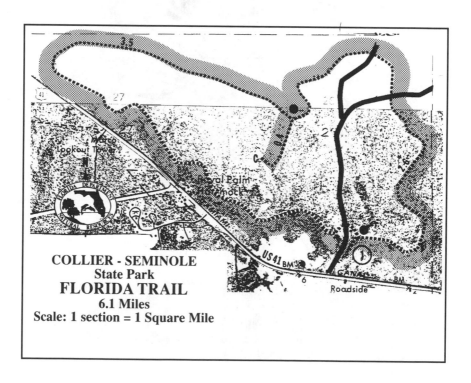

COLLIER - SEMINOLE
State Park
FLORIDA TRAIL
6.1 Miles
Scale: 1 section = 1 Square Mile

Collier County

Okeechobee East and Southeast

Location
The northern terminus is at the South Florida Water Management District's Okee-tantie Recreation Area on SR 78, about six miles southwest of Okeechobee on the north shore of the lake at the Kissimmee River. The southern terminus is in Clewiston on US 27. Trail mileage data and maps are divided at Canal Point about four miles north of Pahokee State Park.

Type of Hiking
Hiking is high and dry on the dikes with no shade and with long, straight stretches, sometimes reaching the horizon. There are great views of the Everglades and lakeshore wildlife. Best views of the lake are along the dike's west rim. The trail leaves the dike where canals intersect with the lake. Hikers cross the canal bridges, then return to the dike. The trail is long and penetrates into remote areas. Be prepared and plan carefully.

Water
There is potable water at communities and facilities along the route. Boil, filter or treat lake and canal water. It may contain dangerous agricultural runoff.

Conveniences
Supplies: Okeechobee, Pahokee, Canal Point, Clewiston, South Bay
Mail: Okeechobee 33472, Pahokee 33476, South Bay 33493,
        Clewiston 33440
Motels: At communities above and at Cypress Lodge, Port Mayaca.
Campgrounds: Pahokee State Park, Belle Glade City Campground,
        Okee-tantie

Emergency
Palm Beach County Sheriff: 407-837-2000
Martin County Sheriff: 407-283-1300
Okeechobee County Sheriff: 813-763-3117
Corps of Engineers, Clewiston: 813-983-8101

Precautions
Wear protection from the sun and be prepared for mosquitoes. Camping is permitted on the dike at designated sites. Call the Corps for information. Hikers can call Slim's Fish Camp on Torry Island--407-996-8750--to arrange for ferry pickup to bypass Belle Glade. Alternatively, hikers can cross a bridge to the island and arrange to be dropped off by boat.

Description

This trail is on the Herbert Hoover Dike along the east shore of Lake Okeechobee. The views of the lakeshore and surrounding areas are striking. You may see racoons, foxes, possums, armadillos and alligators, as well as all kinds of wading birds. On Christmas 1837, the "Battle of Lake Okeechobee" was fought at Nubbins Slough. Eight hundred American troops and state militia, commanded by Colonel Zachary Taylor, fought 400 Seminole and black warriors near the lake shore. Flood gates were built at Belle Glade after the devastating hurricane of 1928, in which 2,000 people drowned.

Trail Data - Okeechobee East

Mileage S to N		Mileage N to S
36.2	North terminus at Okee-tantie Recreation Area on east side of Kissimmee River. Water, parking, camping.	0.0
36.0	Pass gate across dike.	0.2
32.2	Pass access road to county park at lakeside. Junction of dike with Taylor Creek Road. Follow Taylor Creek Lodge Road.	4.0
30.0	Cross Taylor Creek on bridge. Restaurants, stores nearby.	6.2
29.8	Trail turns at dike-access road junction at Taylor Creek.	6.4
29.6	Trail on dike. Lock, pump station 113.	6.6
27.3 ⑥	Cross Nubbin Slough (C-59) on US 441 bridge (or use crawl-through in fence to cross structure). Junction with 9.0 mile trail to north side of Okeechobee following the northwest side of L-63. Trail turns at dike-access road junction. Trail on dike. No mainland access between here and Henry Creek.	8.9
24.0	Cross boat lock service bridge at Henry Creek. Trail on dike. No mainland access between here and Chancy Bay.	12.2
17.3	Cross Chancy Bay service bridge. Water, camping at J&S Fish Camp. Trail on dike. No mainland access between here and Chancy Bay.	18.9
9.7 ⑤	Junction with US 441 bridge over St. Lucie Canal at Port Mayaca with store, guest house 0.25 mile south of bridge.	26.5
4.1	Pass Sand Cut. Trail on dike. Cross five small inlets.	32.1
0.0	Trail follows dike access road through Canal Point. Follow highway for groceries. Water.	36.2

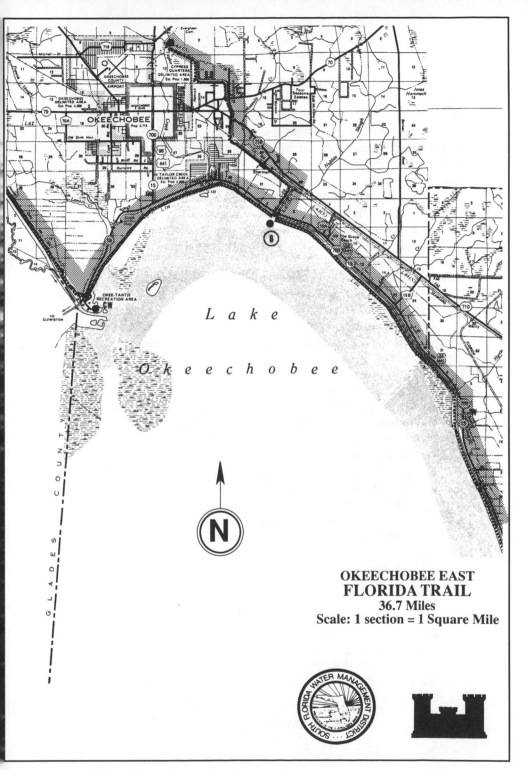

OKEECHOBEE EAST
FLORIDA TRAIL
36.7 Miles
Scale: 1 section = 1 Square Mile

Okeechobee, Martin, Palm Beach Counties

Trail Data - Okeechobee Southeast

Mileage S to N		Mileage N to S
29.2	Trail follows dike. Road to Canal Point. Groceries, water.	0.0
28.9	Trail follows unpaved dike access road through gate. Trail on dike.	0.3
26.1	Pass gate.	3.1
25.7 ④	North boundary of Pahokee State Park at Tower Road. Camping. Restaurant, drug store, groceries in Pahokee.	3.5
25.1	South boundary of Pahokee State Park on dike. Gate. 4.1	
21.5	Pass 2 gates. Glades Airport to northeast. North end of Rim Canal.	7.7
19.5	Trail passes gate at Rardin Park. Water, restrooms. 9.7	
17.5	Pass two gates and road.	11.7
15.9 ③	Cross SR 717 bridge for Torry Island, Belle Glade Marina Campground, groceries, camping. Slim's Fish Camp boat ferry to dike on south side of hurricane gates. Alternate: Through Belle Glade via SR 717 for 9 miles.	13.3
15.1 ②	Trail passes gates. Picnic tables. Access road to US 27.	14.1
9.1	Trail through Lake Harbor. Water, picnic tables, restrooms at the park. Junction of Miami Canal levee and Hoover Dike. Ask at Corps of Engineer gatekeeper's office for use of phone to call Slim's for ferry if hiking north.	20.1
5.2	Pass pump station.	24.0
4.2	Pass campground on south side of US 27.	25.0
1.1	Pass Clewiston city line. Access to highway.	28.1
0.0 ①	South terminus at Clewiston floodgate structure at US 27 bridge. Pass Corps of Engineers equipment yard. Trail resumes on dike after 1/2 mile. Map continues on page 32.	29.2

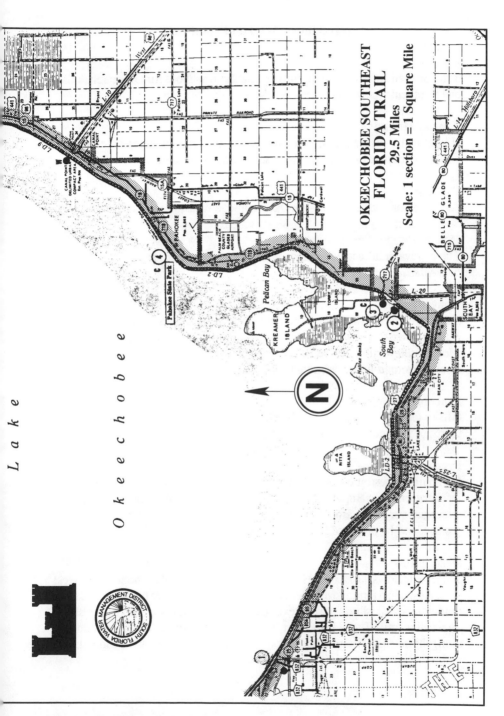

OKEECHOBEE SOUTHEAST
FLORIDA TRAIL
29.5 Miles
Scale: 1 section = 1 Square Mile

Hendry, Palm Beach Counties

Okeechobee West and Southwest

Location
The northern and southern termini are the same as those for Okeechobee East and Southeast (page 25).

Type of Hiking
Hiking is dry on the Herbert Hoover Dike. Some road walking is required to cross canal inlets to the lake. The trail is long and remote.

Parking
At Clewiston, advise police. At Okee-tantie, advise appropriate personnel.

Water
There is water at recreation areas. *Rim Canal and pump station water should be treated.*

Conveniences
Supplies: Clewiston, Moore Haven, Lakeport and Okeechobee
Mail: Clewiston 33440, Moore Haven 33471, Okeechobee 33472
Motels: Clewiston, Moore Haven, Okeechobee
Public Campgrounds: Okee-tantie

Emergency
Glades County Sheriff: 813-946-1600
Corps of Engineers, Clewiston: 813-983-8101

Precautions
Camping is permitted on the dike at designated sites. Call the Corps for information. No camping is permitted within the perimeters of pump stations, water gates or locks. Boil, filter or treat all ground water. Wear protection from the sun, and be prepared for mosquitoes.

Description
This trail follows the Herbert Hoover Dike around Lake Okeechobee on its west side. Australian pine and melaleuca forests and the presence of marshlands and numerous small islands prevent extensive views of the lake. There is no shade on the dike trail. The only trees are at the base of the levee. Birds are abundant along the dikes, with egrets and herons dominant. Kites, hawks, meadowlarks, and red-winged blackbirds are often seen.

Trail Data - Okeechobee West

Mileage S to N			Mileage N to S
21.9	(5)	North terminus at Okee-tantie Recreation Area on east side of Kissimmee River. Water, parking, camping. Trail continues on east side of Lake Okeechobee. Trail route crosses Kissimmee River on SR 78 bridge.	0.0
19.0		Pass Buckhead Ridge pump station.	2.9
12.2		Trail route crosses Indian Prairie Canal on highway. Pass pump station.	9.7
5.0		Pass Bear Beach pump station.	16.9
3.9	(4)	Trail route crosses Harney Pond Canal. Food, drink and gas on north side of canal.	18.0
1.8		Pass pump station at Lakeport Canal. RV resort north on SR 78 near Lakeport.	20.1
0.0	(3)	Trail route (on dike) junction with highway. Cross canal and Curry Island slough area on SR 78. Pass Sportsman's Village Access Area.	21.9

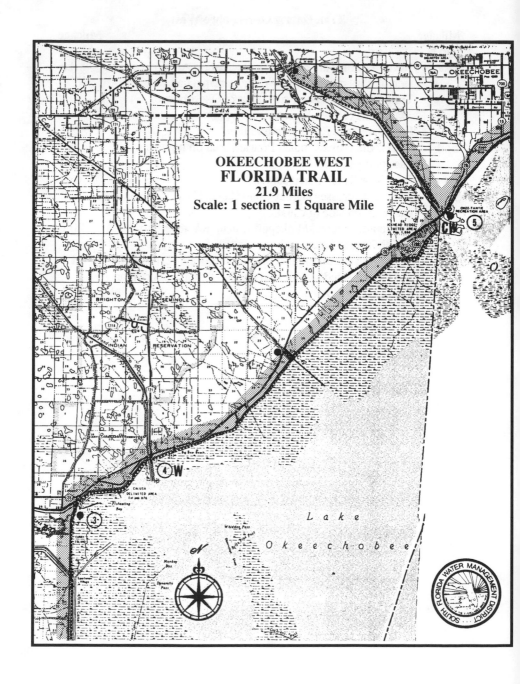

OKEECHOBEE WEST
FLORIDA TRAIL
21.9 Miles
Scale: 1 section = 1 Square Mile

Glades, Hendry, Okeechobee Counties

Trail Data - Okeechobee Southwest

Mileage
S to N

Mileage
N to S

S to N		N to S
20.5	Dike trail joins SR 78. Pass Moore Haven Recreation Area. Camping, snacks store. Cross two earthen bridges. Cross Caloosahatchee River (Cross State Canal) on US 27 bridge.	0.0
11.3	Moore Haven Flood Gate.	9.2
5.9 ②	Pass Liberty Point, Uncle Joe's Fish Camp. Cabins, food. Trail on dike.	14.6
0.8	Trail route (on dike) junction with northwest corner of parking lot. Route turns at Lake Okeechobee access point opposite marina. Pass Angler's Marina. Store, campsites. Follow US 27 for 0.4 miles.	19.7
0.0 ①	South terminus at US 27 bridge (Clewiston). Junction with trail on east side of Lake Okeechobee, and the Highlands-Okeechobee trail to the north.	20.5

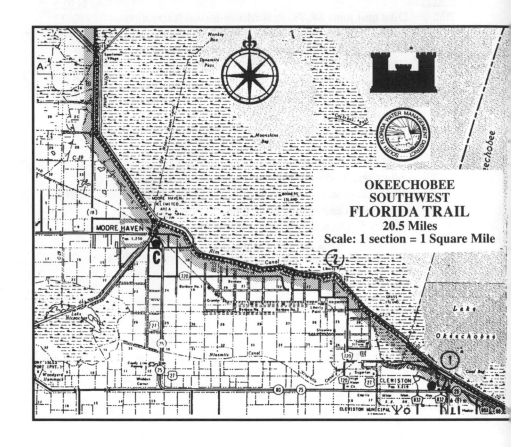

OKEECHOBEE
SOUTHWEST
FLORIDA TRAIL
20.5 Miles
Scale: 1 section = 1 Square Mile

Glades, Hendry, Okeechobee Counties

Highlands - Okeechobee

Location
The southern terminus is at the South Florida Water Management District's Okee-tantie Recreation Area on SR 78, six miles southwest of Okeechobee city on the north shore of Lake Okeechobee at the Kissimmee River (C-38). The temporary northern terminus is at the SR 70 bridge at the Kissimmee River.

Type of Hiking
The trail goes through an open area along the east side of the Kissimmee River channel.

Parking
Park at Okee-tantie, and advise appropriate personnel. Park at the northern terminus at your own risk.

Water
There is potable water at Okee-tantie and at a faucet on the north side of the S65E structure manager's home. Boil, filter or treat river water.

Conveniences
Supplies: Okeechobee
Mail: Okeechobee 34973
Motels: Okeechobee
Public Campgrounds: Okee-tantie Recreation Area

Emergency
Okeechobee County Sheriff: 813-763-3117

Precautions
Wear protection from the sun.

Description
This nine-mile spur follows the east bank of the Kisssimmee River channel on levees along the channel to Lake Okeechobee. The meanders of the original river can still be seen to the west. As in most open areas near water, wading birds are plentiful and good views of the river floodplain are constant along this hike. Sandhill cranes can often be seen feeding in pastures to the east. A swimming break in the river is available at the SR 70 bridge. Look for a planted grove of Indian Rosewood trees on the east side of this section. Hikers should stay on the higher levee elevation because the channel bank is weedy and muddy.

Trail Data - Highlands-Okeechobee Section
(see map on page 32)

(see map on page 32)

Mileage S to N		Mileage N to S
9.1	Temporary northern terminus at SR 70 bridge at Kissimmee River. Camping available in oak hammock and swimming at bridge. Trail along channel on Water Management District right-of-way.	0.0
7.8	Cross canal on footbridge.	1.3
7.7	Pass S65E structure manager's house through rear yard.	1.4
4.9	Pass water control structure and gate.	4.2
4.7	Trail turns passing boat launch area near water control structure.	4.4
1.1	Pass culvert.	8.0
0.1	Cross gate on dike.	9.0
0.0 ⑤	South terminus at Okee-tantie recreation area on east side of Kissimmee River. Water, parking, camping. Trail along channel on Water Management District right-of-way.	9.1

The length of the trail around Lake Okeechobee tests the psyche as well as the physique. It gives a close-up view of the immense works of man that have been put in place to tame the "River of Grass." Hikers will learn the price this delicate, beautiful area has had to pay to ensure the continued growth of the huge megalopolis to the east.

Corbett Wildlife Management Area

Location
The east terminus begins at the Everglades Youth Camp on Stumper's Grade road, 3.8 miles south of the SR 710 entrance to Corbett WMA, which is 11 miles northwest of the intersection of the Old Military Trail and SR 710 in West Palm Beach. The west terminus is only reachable by trail.

Type of Hiking
The trail goes through pine flatwoods, wet prairie and cypress meadow.

Parking
Park at the trail registration box near the trailhead.

Water
Water is available at the Everglades Youth Camp. Be sure to carry enough. Boil, filter or treat all ground water.

Conveniences
Supplies: at Palm Beach Gardens on SR 710
Mail: North Palm Beach 33408
Motels: Palm Beach Gardens, North Palm Beach
Public Campgrounds: Jonathan Dickinson State Park

Emergencies
Palm Beach County Sheriff: 407-471-2000
Game and Fish Commission: 800-432-2046

Precautions
Wear safety orange during general hunting season.

Restrictions
Hikers must have a WMA permit to use the area. See Corbett WMA regulations. Build campfires only in designated areas.

Description
The trail wanders through pine flatwoods, palmetto and shrubs. You may have to wade through the low areas during the rainy season. During late spring and early summer, look for wildflowers all along the trail. Deer,wild hogs and many small animals live here, as do many types of birds from bald eagles to hummingbirds. Look also for a colony of bluebirds and for red-cockaded woodpeckers. In the west area, the trail crosses an Indian mound.

Trail Data - Corbett Section

Mileage E to W			Mileage W to E
0.0	①	East terminus at Everglades Youth Camp. Parking, water.	14.0
0.8		Trail crosses wet prairie.	13.2
1.2		Cross power line and unimproved road.	12.8
2.0		Cross unimproved road.	12.0
3.0		Trail passes north side of wet prairie.	11.0
5.0		Pass trail to campsite on tree island to the south. No water.	9.0
7.0		Trail crosses cypress meadow.	7.0
7.8		Cross South Grade road.	6.2
9.0		Cross canal.	5.0
10.0		Cross abandoned farm field.	4.0
10.5		Cross unimproved road.	3.5
11.0		Pass campsite. No water.	3.0
11.2		Cross canal on unimproved road.	2.8
11.8		Cross unimproved road near edge of abandoned farm field.	2.2
13.0		Cross Indian mound.	1.0
14.0		West boundary of Corbett WMA at fence.	0.0

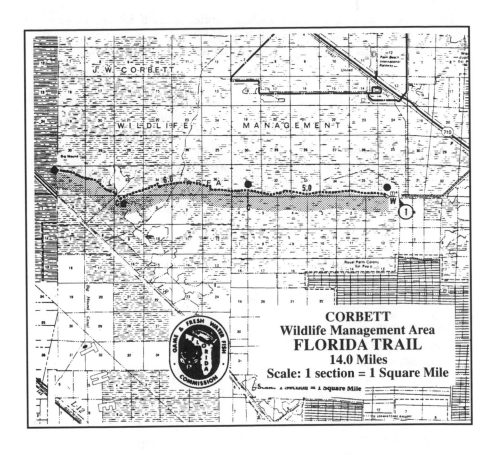

CORBETT
Wildlife Management Area
FLORIDA TRAIL
14.0 Miles
Scale: 1 section = 1 Square Mile

Palm Beach County

DuPuis Reserve State Forest

Location
The northern terminus is at the trailhead/parking area off SR 76, approximately six miles west of its junction with SR 710 at Indiantown. The southern terminus is at DuPuis Grade, now accessible only by trail.

Type of Hiking
Both day hikes and longer backpacking trips are possible on this standard FTA orange-blazed trail. The trails have been developed in a stacked loop (four loops) system offering hikers a choice of hikes ranging from 4.3 to 15.5 miles. Extensive areas may be wet during the rainy season, and hog rootings may make certain trail reaches somewhat strenuous to walk.

Parking
Park at the trailhead off SR 76.

Water
Carry enough water for your trip. All ground and well water must be boiled, filtered or treated. Plans have been made to dig a well at the campsite. Check with the Forest Supervisor, 407-924-8021.

Conveniences
Supplies: At Indiantown on SR 710
Mail: Indiantown 33456
Motels: Port Mayaca, Indiantown, Stuart
Public Campgrounds: Jonathan Dickinson State Park, Pahokee State Park,
        Belle Glade recreaction area, Okee-Tantie recreation area

Emergencies
Martin County Sheriff: 407-220-7000
Palm Beach County Sheriff: 407-471-2000
Game and Fish Commission: 404-683-0748

Precautions
Carry plenty of water, and treat any water you get on the reserve. Sign the trail register. Lock your car. As you should before embarking on any hiking trip, advise someone of your itinerary. Get a camping permit and consult the bulletin board at the trailhead for current regulations.

Restrictions

Camp only at the designated site. You must have a permit to camp overnight. Call the forest headquarters for information about permits. Guns, dogs and trapping devices are prohibited, and vehicles are restricted to the trailhead/ parking area. The reserve is closed on the dates of scheduled hunts.

Description

The reserve encompasses approximately 21,900 acres in western Palm Beach and Martin Counties and was purchased by the South Florida Water Management District under Florida's Save Our Rivers Program. A mosaic of pine flatwoods, ponds, cypress domes, wet prairies, and cabbage palm hammocks, the reserve is home to a variety of native plants and animals, including a number of endangered and threatened species. Occasional sightings of the endangered Florida panther have been reported. A number of Indian mounds are located in the southwestern portion of the property along what was once the northeastern edge of the historic Everglades.

In addition to hiking and backpacking, the reserve is open to horseback riding, birding, photography, and limited hunting. Management of the fish and wildlife resources of the reserve and the regulation of public use is the responsibility of the Florida Game and Fresh Water Fish Commission. Roadway maintenance, prescribed burning, exotic plant control and the development of general recreation opportunities are handled by the Florida Division of Forestry. The District will concentrate its efforts on the management of the reserve's water resources, including the restoration and revitalization of extensive wetland areas drained by the former owners for pastureland.

Trail data - DuPuis Reserve State Forest

Mileage Counterclockwise		Mileage Clockwise
15.3 ①	North terminus at trailhead off SR 76.	0.0
14.8	Junction trailhead spur and DuPuis Grade (E-W leg).	0.5
14.7	Trailhead spur passes "Governor's House".	0.6
14.6	Junction trailhead spur, Loop 1E and Loop 1W.	0.7
14.5	Loop 1E crosses horse trail.	0.8
14.2	Loop 1E crosses fence.	1.1
13.6	Loop 1E crosses horse trail.	1.7
13.4	Juntion Loop 1E, cross trail and Loop 2E.	1.9
13.3	Loop 2E crosses fence.	2.0
13.0	Loop 2E crosses ditch.	2.3
12.2	Junction Loop 2E & side trail to picnic area.	3.1
12.1	Loop 2E crosses fence. Junction cross trail and Loop 3E.	3.2
10.9	Loop 3E crosses fence.	4.4
10.7	Loop 3E passes Boot Lake.	4.6
9.9	Junction Loop 3E, cross trail and Loop 4E.	5.4
9.7	Loop 4E crosses fence.	5.6
9.1	Loop 4E crosses woods road.	6.2
8.4	Loop 4E crosses fence.	6.9
8.1	Loop 4E crosses ditch.	7.2
8.0	Junction Loop 4E, DuPuis Grade spur, and Loop 4W.	7.3
7.9	Loop 4W crosses ditch.	7.4
7.6	Loop 4W crosses fence.	7.7
6.0	Junction Loop 4W and woods road.	9.3
5.8	Loop 4W crosses fence. Junction loop 4W and side trail to campsite.	9.5
5.7	Junction Loop 4W, cross trail and Loop 3W.	9.6
4.6	Loop 3W crosses fence. 10.7	
3.6	Loop 3W crosses ditch.	11.7
3.5	Loop 3W crosses ditch.	11.8
3.0	Junction Loop 3W cross trail and Loop 2W.	12.3
2.9	Loop 2W crosses fence.	12.4
2.7	Loop 2W crosses horse trail.	12.6
1.8	Junction Loop 2W, cross trail and Loop 1W.	13.5
1.5	Loop 1W crosses ditch.	13.8
1.0	Loop 1W crosses ditch.	14.3
0.7	Junction Loop 1W trailhead spur and Loop 1F.	14.6
0.6	Trailhead spur passes "Governor's House".	14.7
0.5	Trailhead spur crosses ditch. Junction with DuPuis Grade (E-W).	14.8
0.0	North terminus at trailhead of SR 76.	15.3

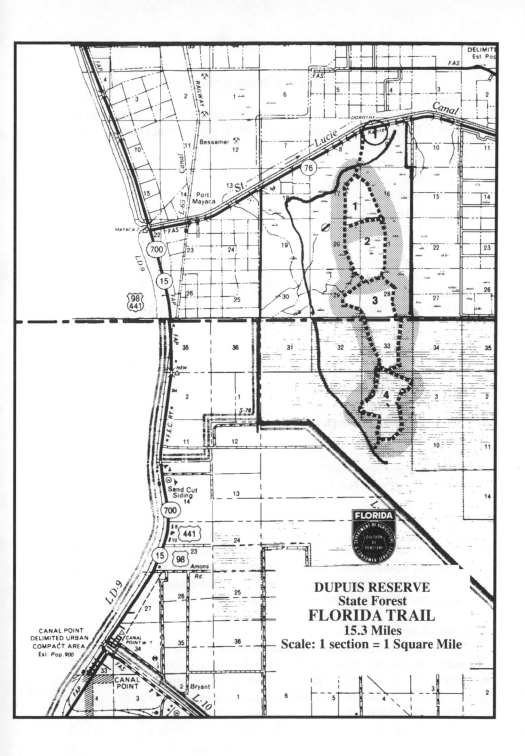

DUPUIS RESERVE
State Forest
FLORIDA TRAIL
15.3 Miles
Scale: 1 section = 1 Square Mile

Martin, Palm Beach Counties

43

Jonathan Dickinson State Park

Location
The park is in Martin County, 3.5 miles north of Jupiter, Florida on the west side of US 1. The terminus is at the north end of the park entrance station parking lot.

Type of Hiking
The trail goes through sand pine scrub and pine flatwoods. You may have to wade in parts in rainy seasons. Obtain a trail brochure at the entrance.

Parking
Hikers are required to park at the entrance station parking lot.

Water
There is water at the campground and the picnic area. Water from the well along the trail is not potable and must be treated.

Conveniences
Supplies: In Jupiter, along US 1, and at park concession.
Mail: Hobe Sound 33455 Jupiter 33458
Motels: Jupiter and along US 1
Public Campgrounds: In park

Emergency
Martin County Sheriff: 407-283-1300
Park Manager: 407-546-2771

Precautions
Reservations for camping are provided to a limited number of people, first come first served. The park address is 14800 SE Federal Highway, Hobe Sound, FL 33455. Register at the entrance. Notify them when you return. Camp only in the designated campsites. Leave the entrance six hours before sundown to reach the campsite before dark. Leave the campsite by noon.

Restrictions
The campsite is limited to eight persons per night. Pets, bicycles, and motorized equipment are prohibited on the trail. Use of downed or dead wood for campfires is prohibited. Do not disturb plants or animals. Firearms are prohibited. The park is open from eight a.m. to sundown. The gates will be closed if the park is full.

Description

Surrounding the beautiful Loxahatchee River and the cypress swamps of Kitching Creek, this 10,000 acre park has varied vegetation and is home to over 700 species of animals. Canoeing and bicycling are available. The park provides a vivid example of sand pine germination. Hikers will see the evidence of wildfires, which open pine cones to release seeds. In the sand pine scrub communities, look for the towhees and scrub jays. The hills are actually sand dunes of an ocean shore long since receded to the east. The "stumps" area is evidence of the logging done twice before in this century, in 1900 and 1940. Kitching Creek is named for Captain Kitching, whose boat plied the waters of the Indian River and Hobe Sound during the 1880s. Susan Kitching, his sister, purchased this property in 1886 for $1.25 per acre.

Trail Data - Jonathan Dickinson State Park

There are two campsites, one 5.6 miles from the trailhead on the east loop trail, and the other 9.4 miles west on the Kitching Creek trail.

Mileage Clockwise			Mileage Counterclockwise
9.4	①	East terminus is inside park near the park entrance station. Trail passes through sand pine scrub area for 2.0 miles.	0.0
7.4		Trail crosses park servive road.	2.0
7.2		Cross Old Dixie Highway (original US 1). Cross Florida East Coast RR.	2.2
6.9		Trail passes small marsh on south side. Trail passes through mixed slash and sand pine.	2.5
5.1		Cross concrete culvert under live oak tree.	4.3
4.6		Cross wooden bridge.	4.8
4.1	②	Pass well on NW side of trail. Treat water. Get water here for east campsite. Intersection with west campsite trail. Turn east at intersection for Scrub Jay Campsite.	5.3
3.7		Scrub Jay campsite (no water). Camp only within area designated by trees with white ring around trunk. Ground fires only in the fire ring. Trail continues east.	5.6
3.6		Turn south.	5.7
2.6		Trail leaves road, continues south through pine/palmetto.	6.7
2.0		Trail crosses main park road. Trail continues south on fire road.	7.3
1.7	③	Trail turns southeast through wooded area.	7.7
1.5		Trail turns east on fire lane.	7.9
1.1		Cross Rainy Slough wooden footbridge. Trail continues southeast.	8.3
0.9		Intersect sand road parallel to railroad tracks.	8.5
0.5		Cross RR tracks on diagonal. Trail continues for short distance south on east side of RR.	8.9
0.4		Turn east on old road.	9.0
0.3		Turn south. Follow lake perimeter.	9.1
0.1		Turn north, then east to park gate.	9.3
0.0		Register box. Please sign out/in.	9.4

Trail Data - Kitching Creek Trail

Mileage W to E		Description	Mileage E to W
4.0	(2)	At intersection turn west for Kitching Creek campsite. Trail follows powerline.	0.0
3.6		Trail passes through low pine flatwoods. Possible wading.	1.4
3.0	(4)	Cross 2-lane horse trail. Give horses right-of-way.	1.5
1.6		Cross canal on wooden bridge.	1.6
1.5		Cross Kitching Creek on wooden bridge.	3.0
1.4		Trail parallels west side of Kitching Creek for 1.4 mile.	3.6
0.0	(5)	West terminus. Campsites, well (treat water), latrine.	4.0

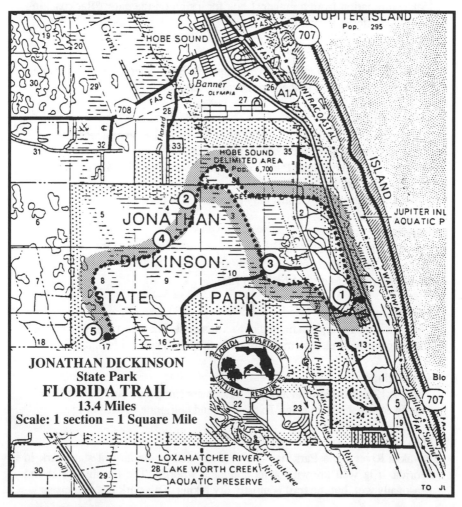

JONATHAN DICKINSON
State Park
FLORIDA TRAIL
13.4 Miles
Scale: 1 section = 1 Square Mile

Martin County

Myakka River State Park

Location
Myakka River State Park is located off SR 72, approximately 15 miles east of Sarasota.

Type of Hiking
The terrain is flat and mostly dry, with pine and palmetto landscape, oak hammocks and sloughs.

Parking
Park at the starting point, which is 0.2 miles from the main park road. Get the lock combination from a ranger. Look for a sign on the gate: "Backpacking Trail - Register at Park Office."

Water
Get water from wells at primitive campsites. Boil, filter or treat this water. There is potable water at the park headquarters.

Conveniences
Supplies: Limited supplies at park concession stand. Convenience store 9
            miles west on SR 72 at I-75 overpass.
Mail: Myakka River State Park 13207 SR 72 Sarasota, FL 34241
Motels: Sarasota or Arcadia
Public Campgrounds: Cabins may be reserved in park.

Emergency
Park Manager: 813-361-6511
Sarasota County Sheriff: 813-951-5800
Manatee County Sheriff: 813-746-7121

Precautions
The park opens at eight a.m. and closes at sunset. There is a fee for backpack camping on the trail. The trail is blazed white with side trails blazed blue.

Restrictions
There is 12 person limit at any one wilderness campsite. Build campfires only in established fire rings. Extinguish and obliterate fires after use.

Description
Myakka River State Park has 29,000 acres and is the largest state park in Florida. It is well known for its abundant wildlife. The terrain is flat and seasonally wet, but the trail is mostly dry hiking. This park has numerous

ponds, marshes, swamps and streams, and the 7,500 acre wilderness preserve is still like the Florida discovered by early explorers. Myakka Trail meanders through hammocks of live oak and cabbage palm, across open palmetto flatwoods and along small marshes. Deer, turkey, otter, wild hogs and bobcats inhabit this park, but hikers have to be lucky, quiet, and knowledgeable of animal habits to see them. There are also eagles, sandhill cranes, ospreys and alligators along with most types of Florida waterfowl. Florida panthers used to live in this area, but there are probably none left now. The park headquarters has a museum, native programs, a boat ride and brochures on the park wildlife. There are remains of pioneer settlements and old cattle camps in the park

The trail has five campsites: Bee Island, Honore, Panther Point, Prairie and Oak Grove. The best time to hike Myakka is in the late fall and early spring, the drier seasons in this part of Florida.

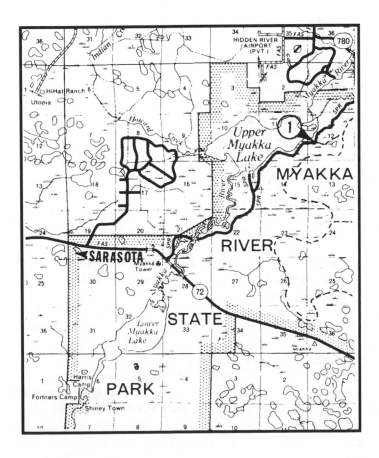

Trail Data - Myakka River State Park

Mileage Clockwise		Mileage Counterclockwise
(1)	Access from main park road 0.3 miles N of Bird Walk. Use chained gate. See general information. Drive E to 2nd chain for parking. Follow blazes for 0.2 miles NE to main loop trail.	
33.3	Blue-blazed access trail junction with white-blazed Bee Island loop.	0.0
29.3	Junction with blue-blazed 2-mile Bee Island Loop-Honore. Loop Cross Trail. Campsite & scenic trails junction 1 mile via cross trail. Campsite & well 0.1 mile N of cross trail. Well & historic cattle dip vat 0.2 mile S of cross trail.	4.0
27.8	Trail makes perpendicular crossing with power line. Trail also crosses two horse trails in area.	5.5
25.9	Trail junction with 0.1-mile blue-blazed trail to Honore campsite. Pass well at entrance to camp area.	8.4
23.5	Honore Loop trail crosses power line.	9.8
22.0	Honore & Deer Prairie Loops junction with 0.8-mile blue-blaze north-south Bobcat Cross Trail.	11.3
20.5	Deer Prairie Loop trail junction with 0.1-mile blue-blazed trail to Panther Point campsite. Pass well at entrance to campsite.	12.8
17.0	Deer Prairie & East Loops junction with 1.5-mile blue-blazed north-south Slough Cross Trail.	16.3
13.9	Trail crosses abandoned railroad grade.	19.4
12.5	East Loop trail junction with 0.2-mile blue-blazed trail to Prairie Campsite. Well & historic cattle dip vat.	20.8
10.1	Deer Prairie & East Loops junction with blue-blazed 1.5-mile north-south Slough Cross Trail.	23.2
9.7	Deer Prairie Loop trail junction with 0.3-mile blue-blazed trail to Oak Grove campsite. Pass well on right when entering oak grove.	23.6
6.7	Honore & Deer Prairie Loops junction with 0.8-mile north-south blue-blazed Bobcat Cross Trail.	26.6
5.0	Junction with blue-blazed 2-mile Bee Island Loop-Honore Loop Cross Trail. Campsite & scenic trails junction 1 mile via cross trail. Campsite & well 0.1 mile N of cross trail. Historic cattle dip vat 0.2 mile S of cross trail.	28.3
0.0	Blue-blazed access trail junction with white-blazed Bee Island loop.	33.3

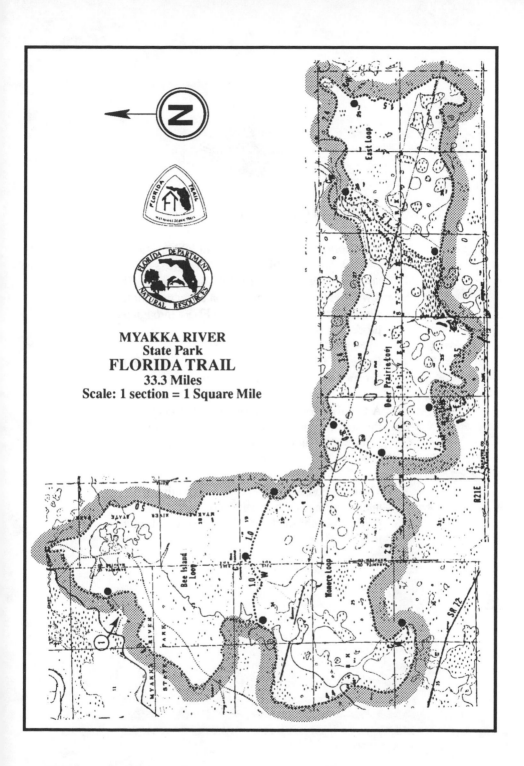

MYAKKA RIVER
State Park
FLORIDA TRAIL
33.3 Miles
Scale: 1 section = 1 Square Mile

Manatee, Sarasota Counties

FLORIDA NATIONAL SCENIC TRAIL

The Florida National Scenic Trail (abbreviated as FNST) was established by Congress as an amendment to the National Trail Systems Act. The law provides for the designation of sections of the Florida Trail as segments of the FNST through the process of certification.

Eleven of the trails in this book are or soon will be certified as National Scenic Trails.

A Certification Plan, signed by the managing authority, the maintaining organization, and the landowner(s) must be completed for each certification.

The U. S. Forest Service is the coordinating agency and must approve the certification plans. The certification is published and signs are erected on the trail.

CENTRAL FLORIDA

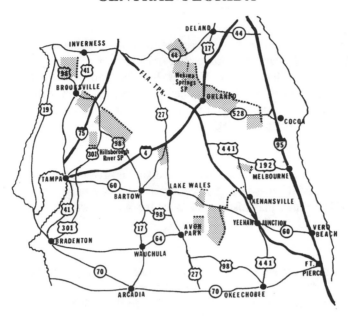

This area covers the part of Florida extending from the northern edge of the Everglades to the southern edge of Ocala National Forest. It offers more hiking on loop trails in state parks and wildlife management areas than any other region in the state, providing convenient situations for day-hikers or for weekend hikers who have only one automobile and cannot arrange transportation between end points of a hike on a through-trail.

The terrain and vegetation in the region vary widely. Almost every type of walking experience can be found somewhere in the area; swamps, prairies, riverbanks, savannahs, oak and palm hammocks, caves, and pine and turkey oak forests. The Wekiwa Springs State Park trail touches or crosses crystal clear springs and streams and passes through dense jungle. Central Florida rests on a bed of limestone. As the limestone dissolves, caves and sinkholes appear, and streams disappear into the ground. A sinkhole achieved notoriety in 1981 by consuming part of the city of Winter Park.

The flat areas of this region are cow country with a history that rivals the Wild West. Many Florida cowboys used whips instead of lariats because of the heavy undergrowth. They herded cattle by cracking the whip, which some say is the origin of the term "Florida Cracker."

Kissimmee River

Location
The Kissimmee River trail is on the west side of the Kissimmee River from SR 60 to Bluff Hammock Road, five miles north of Lorida. The north terminus is 19 miles west of Yeehaw Junction and seven miles east of Indian Lakes Estates on SR 60, immediately west of the Kissimmee River bridge. The south terminus is at the north end of Bluff Hammock Road at water control structure S65B.

Type of Hiking
Kissimmee River offers oak hammock, dike, and river bank walking with wet areas in rainy seasons. This section is one of the most remote areas of the Florida Trail. Part of the trail skirts the Avon Park Air Force Range. Fine vistas and sunsets are common.

Parking
At the north end, enter the River Ranch access road at highway 60. Proceed to the River Ranch security kiosk. Go .3 mile past the kiosk. Turn right and go .8 mile to a fenced-in area. This is the Kicco Wildlife Management Area. Camping is permitted here. At the south end, park at your own risk in the parking areas for lock S65B.

Water
There is potable water at River Ranch, the S65B structure, and from pitcher pumps at Ft. Kissimmee. Treat well, surface and river water.

Conveniences
Supplies: River Ranch, 24700 Highway 60 East, Lake Wales, FL 33853
        1-800-282-7935
Mail: Indian Lakes Estates 33855, Lorida 33857 (or c/o River
        Ranch)
Motels: River Ranch (with restaurant)
Public Campgrounds: Lake Kissimmee State Park

Emergency
USAF Security Police: 813-452-4195
Polk County Sheriff: 813-533-0444
Highlands County Sheriff: 813-385-5111

Precautions:
On the Air Force Range, do not touch anything resembling munitions. Do not leave the blazed trail. The U.S. government assumes no liability for any

injuries incurred by hikers on Avon Park AFB. Sign in at all registers on the trail. Leave all gates as you found them.

Restrictions:
This section of the National Scenic Trail is open to the public. Camp only at designated campsites along the way. During the general hunting season, use only the Ft. Kissimmee campsite on the Avon Park Air Force Range. A minimum of two hikers is required when hiking through the Range. Vehicles may gain access to the range through the East-West road when the Avon Park AFB is open. Call 813-452-4223 for a recording or 813-452-4119 Monday - Friday, 7:30 AM-3:30PM for information.

Description:
This portion of the National Scenic Trail follows both the original Kissimmee River, presently being restored, and the man-made river channel. The terrain is flat. There are some swampy sections where wading may be necessary in wet weather. Along the way, oak hammocks and pine palmetto flatlands alternate and intermingle. The trail passes several places of historic interest, including the ghost town of Kicco, the location of old Fort Kissimmee and the Godwin homestead. Animal life abounds. You may see deer, alligators, eagles, wild hogs, turkeys, hawks and many water birds. Audubon's caracara, a rare, strikingly marked vulture, has been spotted in this area, and there are sandhill cranes.

Trail Data - Kissimmee River

Mileage S to N		Mileage N to S
30.8	North terminus at Kissimmee River bridge on SR 60	0.0
30.3	Trail junction with SR 60 near gate on levee. Trail follows levee for 1.8 miles.Trail turns north and west for .6 mile	0.5
27.9	Cross fence on stile at River Ranch access road.	2.9
26.7	Follow access road to River Ranch Resort entrance kiosk.	4.1
26.4	Follow blazes .3 mile to Kicco Wildlife Management entrance road on right.	4.4
25.6 ①	Go .8 mile to trail head. Parking and overnight camping allowed.	5.2
24.6	Long Hammock campsite. Water in stream 200 yds S of sign.	6.2
23.4	Cross Ice Cream and 8 Mile Slough canals on bridge.	7.4
22.6	Trail nears north gate of cattle pens, then follows fence	8.2
21.8	Pass double blaze on northeast corner post of SFWMD fence. The shell road following the river channel may be more dry than the trail through reclaimed marshland.	9.0

19.5	Pass Owen Godwin homestead at Rattlesnake Hammock.	11.3
18.0	Trail through Kicco. Note sidewalks. Water from old river ox-bow 150 yards from the trail.	12.8
17.1	Pass rancher's campsite in Camp Hammock.	13.7
16.7 ②	Trail junction with flood levee. Camping in oak hammock here.Water available from slough drainage. Blue-blazed trail goes around Tick Island (3 miles) and intersects main trail south of the campsite.	14.1
16.5	Cross Tick Island Slough on footbridge, west side of levee.	14.3
15.8	Cross fence on stile at county line. USAF-SFWMD boundary.	15.0
14.6	Pass site of house foundation in Orange Hammock.	16.2
12.5	Trail passes 100 ft. blue blazed trail to cattle-dipping vat.	18.3
11.8	Cross cattle guard.	19.0
11.5	Pass Ft. Kissimmee Cemetery; North boundary of camping zone.	19.3
11.0 ③	Trail crosses Ft. Kissimmee at road end. Well. Latrines.	19.8
10.3	South boundary of designated camping zone.	20.5
7.5	Primitive campsite. No water.	23.3
6.8	Trail crosses Hicks Slough on boardwalk.	24.0
4.2	Route turns on north side of AF Range boundary fence.	26.6
4.0	Cross boundary fence on stile at trail junction with dike. Trail follows dike east-west along south side of boundary dike	26.8
3.3	Route turns at dike direction change across flood control gate. Follows dike along old Kissimmee River meanders.	27.5
2.1	Cross break in dike at drainage ditches.	28.7
0.0 ④	South terminus at S65B Lock Access Road west of lock.	30.8

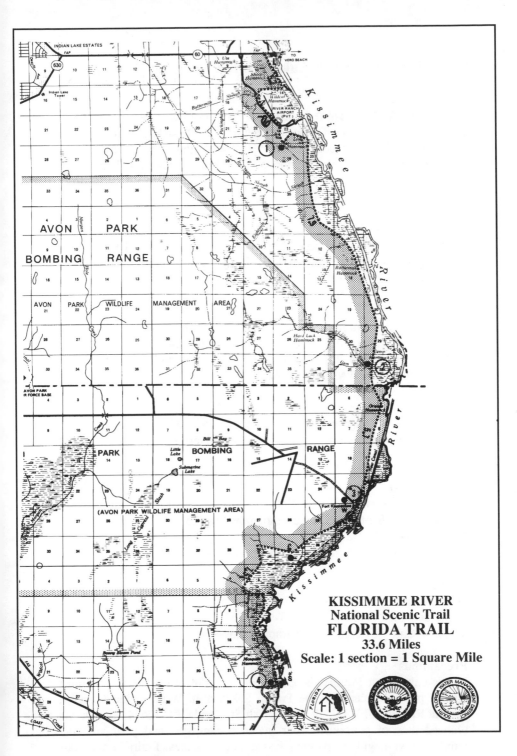

KISSIMMEE RIVER
National Scenic Trail
FLORIDA TRAIL
33.6 Miles
Scale: 1 section = 1 Square Mile

Highlands, Polk Counties

Three Lakes/Prairie Lakes

Location

The Three Lakes trail is in Osceola County on Three Lakes Wildlife Management Area (WMA) land. The north terminus is on US 441, 8.3 miles north of Kenansville. The south terminus is on SR 60, 4.5 miles east of the Kissimmee River bridge. The Prairie Lakes loop trail is within the Prairie Lakes State Preserve.

Type of Hiking

The trail affords level walking through hardwood hammocks, cabbage palm groves, prairie and pine palmetto areas. Wading may be necessary during the wet seasons. Overnight hiking is possible through the entire area or on loops. Short day hiking is ideal.

Parking

Park at the north terminus (along US 441) at your own risk, or park in the hunter's parking area inside the main gate 2.5 miles south of the north terminus. In the Prairie Lakes unit, park near the bridge. At the south terminus, park at the north end of the WMA access road north off SR 60.

Water

There is potable water in a well near the auto bridge, at the Ranger office, at Dry Pond campsite and at the Kissimmee River bridge. Well water and ground water must be treated.

Conveniences

Supplies: Yeehaw Junction (SR 60 and US 441) and Kenansville (SR 523 and US 441) and Lake Marian on SR 523
Mail: Kenansville 32739
Motels: River Ranch, Yeehaw Junction and St. Cloud

Emergency

Osceola County Sheriff: 407-847-5121
Game and Fish Commission: 904-629-8162
Motorist Call Boxes at Trail-Turnpike crossing

Precautions

Prairie Lakes State Preserve is open from eight a.m. until sunset. You must have a permit to camp in the Prairie Lakes unit. Write to the Director, Central Region, GFWFC, 1239 SW 10th St., Ocala, FL 32674. Include the planned date of your visit, your intended campsite, and your auto tag number if you will be parking inside Prairie Lakes. Prairie Lakes has special hunting dates. Check with the Game and Freshwater Fish Commission.

Restrictions
No backpack camping is permitted in the WMA during the general hunting season. Check with the Game and Freshwater Fish Commission to make sure camping is permitted at the time you plan to visit. Camp only in designated areas.

Description
The loop trail in the Prairie Lakes Unit is part of the Florida Recreational Trails System. It lies in a lazy figure eight and wanders through marsh, meadow, hammock and pine forest. As in all Wildlife Management Areas, there is an abundance of animals. Deer are plentiful and hikers often see bald eagles, Audubon's caracara, and the stately sandhill crane.

Trail Data- Three Lakes

Mileage S to N		Mileage N to S
26.6 ①	North terminus on US 441 across from Fontana Lane 2.5 miles north of Three Lakes. WMA maingate is 6.8 miles north of Kenansville. Cross bridge then travel south 30 yards before continuing west on trail.	0.0
26.3	Cross WMA road that connects to loop trail (old trail).	0.3
25.8	Trail crosses swamp area then turns due west for 100 yards, follows fire lane south 100 yards to old RR grade. West on RR grade.	0.8
25.5	Trail follows RR grade for 1.0 mile to WMA Rd. 1, then .4 miles to turnoff. Water .2 mile west.	1.1
24.1	Trail follows fence line around south side of field .8 mile to campground 50 yards north of trail in live oak island.	2.5
23.0	Trail follows RR grade to Williams Rd.	3.6
21.6	Follow Williams Rd. for 1.8 miles.	5.0
19.8 ②	Trail passes through underpass of Florida Turnpike. Follow jeep track for 0.2 mile at 90 degree angle to/from Turnpike. Use Williams Road as alternate path.	6.8
18.6	Trail crosses WMA road 3 loop access road. Cross 0.5 mile of open palmetto area. Trail route alternates on/off jeep road for 0.4 mile	8.0
17.7	Follow spoil bank along ditch.	8.9
17.5	Cross jeep track. Borrow pit to south. Cross pine and palmetto.	9.1
16.9	Cross gate at Williams Road - SR523 junction Trail follows SR 523 for 0.6 mile.	9.7

16.3	Route turns at SR 523 entrance to Prairie Lakes State Preserve.	10.3
16.2	Route follows entrance road for 0.1 mile.	10.4
16.1	Trail junction with entrance road. Note alternate 3.1 mile trail on north side leading to loop junction via Parker Slough.	10.5
15.4	Trail passes through Pole Cypress Pond. Watch for eagles.	11.2
13.7 ③	Trail crosses auto bridge. Register. Campsite, well and latrine are 30 yds. northwest of bridge in hammock. Alternate 3.3 mile trail to south loop junction is south of bridge.	12.9
12.7	Trail passes through edge of Kettle Hammock.	13.9
12.2	Pass Dry Pond campsite. Well, latrine.	14.4
11.4 ④	Trail passes post at junction with alternate 3.3 trail to bridge near Parker Hammock. Cross culvert on jeep road. Follow dike along south edge of Lake Jackson.	15.2
10.5	Cross northeast edge of Jack's Slough Hammock.	16.1
9.9	Cross Preserve fence by climbing gate.	16.7
8.5	Cross Fodderstack Slough bridge. Cross fence on stile on east side of road. Trail follows south edge of Fodderstack Slough for 1.2 miles.	18.1
7.2	Trail on jeep road for .25 mile. Cross north edge of scrub near Godwin Hammock.	19.4
5.8	Blue-blazed trail 150 ft. southeast to campsite (no water).	20.8
4.8	Pass borrow pit, water.	21.8
4.4	Cross south edge of Godwin Hammock. Trail follows jeep road for 0.6 mile.	22.2
3.4	Trail crosses ditch, possible wading. Trail turns at post inside palmetto prairie. Follows seven posts in 330/150 degree bearings across prairie.	23.2
2.5 ⑤	Cross fence on stile. Trail follows fence for 1.3 miles. Trail follows entrance road for 1.2 miles.	24.1
0.0	South terminus at junction of SR 60 and Three Lakes WMA access road.	26.6

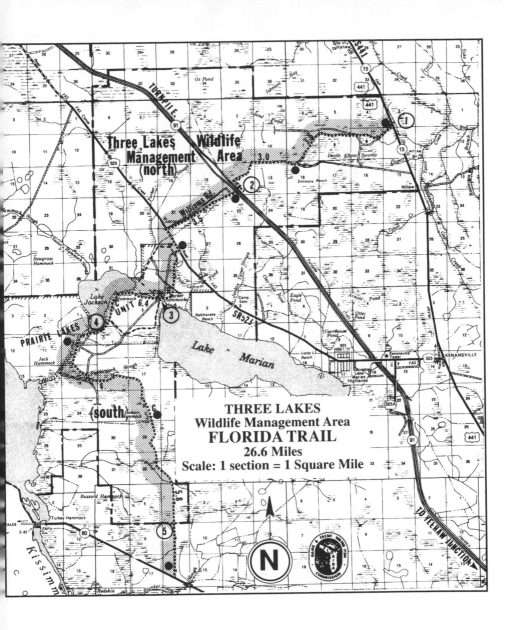

THREE LAKES
Wildlife Management Area
FLORIDA TRAIL
26.6 Miles
Scale: 1 section = 1 Square Mile

Osceola County

Trail Data - Prairie Lakes State Preserve

Mileage Counterclockwise		Mileage Clockwise
	North Loop	
5.5	Bridge, junction of north & south loops. Parking, register.	0.0
5.4	Pass 30 yds. to west of Parker Hammock. Campsite, well, latrine.	0.1
4.3	Trail passes corner of Prairie Lakes fence.	1.2
4.1	Follow east edge of Parker Slough for 0.9 mile.	1.4
3.1	Reach fence. Cross open pine flat.	2.4
2.4 ①	Cross preserve road. Pass around cypress head.	3.1
1.7	Trail passes through Pole Cypress Pond. Pass edge of pine lot.	3.8
1.3	Cross road.	4.2
0.9 ②	Ranger office 100 yards to the west. Water.	4.6
0.7	Trail enters palmetto/pine flat.	4.8
0.4	Edge of Parker Hammock.	5.1
0.0 ③	Bridge, junction of north & south loops. Parking, register.	5.5
	South Loop	
5.7	Bridge, junction of north & south loops. Parking, register.	0.0
5.2	Trail crosses jeep road.	0.4
4.6	Edge of Parker Hammock.	1.0
3.3	Cross road. Pass through Thumb Hammock. Cross meadow.	2.3
2.5	Cross ditch, possible wading.	3.1
2.3 ④	Post marks through-trail and loop trail junction.	3.3
1.5	Pass Dry Pond campsite, well, latrine.	4.1
1.0	Edge of Kettle Hammock. Cross road to Kettle Hammock. Pass through edge of scrub prairie.	4.6
0.5	Trail follows dirt road for 0.25 mile.	5.1
0.3	Cross jeep road.	5.3
0.0	Bridge, junction of north and south loops.	5.7

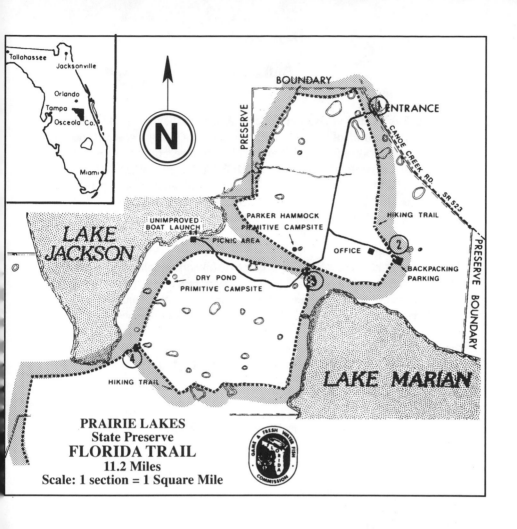

PRAIRIE LAKES
State Preserve
FLORIDA TRAIL
11.2 Miles
Scale: 1 section = 1 Square Mile

Osceola County

Bull Creek

Location
Bull Creek is located in Osceola County. Access to the trail is on Crabgrass Road, six miles south of US 192. The intersection of Crabgrass Road and US 192 is 17 miles southeast of St. Cloud and 19 miles west of the intersection of US 192 and Interstate 95 in Melbourne. Look for the green Wildlife Management Area (WMA) sign. This section is a loop-trail which is also part of the continuous Florida Trail. From the northeast, hikers may enter this section through the Levee 73 trailhead on U.S. 192, 2.3 miles NW of Deer Park.

Type of Hiking
The Florida Trail through Bull Creek is open to hikers throughout the year. The treadway is flat and follows old tramways as it passes through an entire range of ecosystems: flatwoods, cypress-dotted prairie, scrub oak, sand pine, cypress and hardwood swamp. Wading may be necessary in wet seasons.

Parking
Park near the hunt check station on Crabgrass Road and at the Levee 73 trailhead.

Water
There is potable water at the check station, at Little Scrub Camp and at North Camp.

Conveniences
Supplies: St. Cloud, Holopaw, Deer Park
Mail: St. Cloud 32769
Motels: St. Cloud
Public Campgrounds: Moss Park, in Orange County off SR 15

Emergency
Osceola County Sheriff: 407-847-5121
Game & Fish Commission: 904-629-8162

Precautions
Sign in/out at the WMA register box at the check station bulletin board or at the Levee 73 trailhead.

Restrictions
The Bull Creek WMA is open for hunting during Florida's special weapon and general hunting seasons. Check with the Game and Freshwater Fish Commission (904-629-8162) for hunting dates. Backpack camping is permitted year-round along the trail with a permit from the Game and Freshwater Fish Commission's regional office in Ocala. Campfires are permitted only in fire circles at campsites.

Description
The Bull Creek Water Management Area land has been used for livestock grazing, timber harvesting and the production of "naval stores" (turpentine, pitch and resin, which were used to construct and maintain wooden ships). Remnants of these old industries are still scattered about Bull Creek. The Union Cypress Company of Hopkins (Melbourne) operated a system of rail and tram roads to support their logging operation in the cypress swamps along the creeks and sloughs here during the early 20th century. The east leg of this 17-mile loop trail follows the west side of Bull Creek along the old Union Cypress railroad grade. Some ties and hardware can be still be found along the route. There is a small cemetery in Bull Creek, as well as a cattle-dipping vat, flow wells, and "catfaces" (areas on the trunks of trees where the bark has been removed and iron gutters attached to harvest the pitch) on pines in the extreme northeast corner of the property. Remains of a turpentine still and sawmill also are hidden somewhere within the Bull Creek boundaries.

Today, Bull Creek is owned by the St. Johns River Water Management District for use as a retention area for hurricane flood waters, and is leased by the Game and Fresh Water Fish Commission for hunting and recreation. The trail passes through strands of mature cabbage palms, hardwoods and cypress. Wildflowers abound here. The south part of the trail traverses scrub oak and sand pine, and the west leg winds through pine flatwoods and prairie dotted with cypress domes. A variety of plants, birds and other wildlife can be seen amid the several ecosystems along this trail.

Trail Data - Bull Creek

Mileage S to N		Mileage N to S
①	Terminus at hunt check station. Register. Water. Campsite. 0.8 mile access trail follows Crabgrass Road.	
17.0	Junction of Crabgrass Road and Loop Road. Follow Loop Road for 1.8 mile.	0.0
15.2	Trail junction with Loop Road near sabal palm strand. Pass through palm hammock and pine woods.	1.8
14.5	Junction with old RR grade. Trail follows old RR grade.	2.5
14.0	Junction with old RR grade. Trail follows edge of cypress swamp along Bull Creek.	3.0
13.5	Cross Yoke Branch. Follows vehicle trails and Bull Creek wet zone for 1.1 miles.	3.5
12.4	Junction with old RR grade. Follow old RR grade for 0.9 mile.	4.6
11.5	Trail junction with RR grade. Follow vehicle trail. Trail passes through oaks.	5.5
10.9	Junction with old RR grade. Follow RR grade.	6.1
10.2	Junction with old RR grade. Follow vehicle trail.	6.8
9.8	Junction of vehicle trail and Loop Road. Follow Loop Road.	7.2
8.3	Junction of Loop Road and "closed" vehicle road.	8.7
8.0 ②	Pass "Little Scrub" Camping Zone. No water.	9.0
6.8	Cross Nursery Slough on foot plank. Look for baby alligators. Follow vehicle trail for 2.6 miles.	10.2
4.2	Junction of trail on vehicle trail with fire break. Follow fire break and abandoned vehicle trail. Trail follows spoil bank along ditch.	12.8
2.4	Cross ditch.	14.6
1.2	Junction of trail with Loop Road. Trail follows Loop Road for 1.2 miles.	15.8
0.0	Junction of Crabgrass Road and Loop Road.	17.0

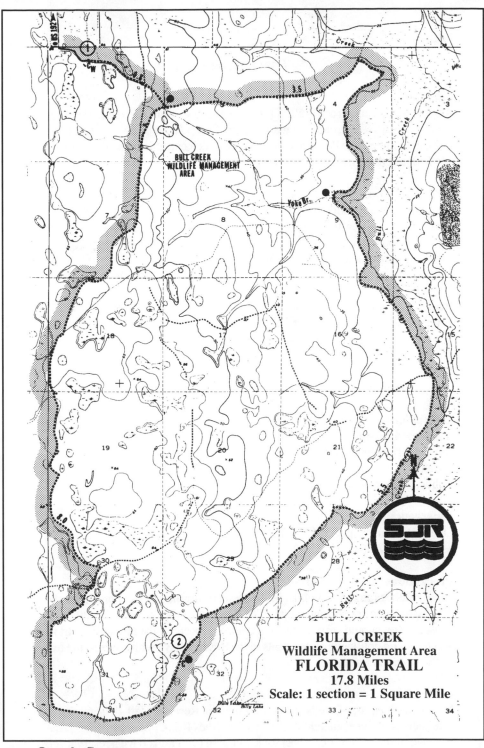

BULL CREEK
Wildlife Management Area
FLORIDA TRAIL
17.8 Miles
Scale: 1 section = 1 Square Mile

Osceola County

67

Tosohatchee

Location
The north terminus is at SR 50, 0.1 mile east of Christmas RV Park. The south terminus is at SR 520, one mile west of the St. Johns River bridge. The entrance to Tosohatchee State Reserve is on Taylor Creek Road 2.5 miles miles north of SR 520 and three miles south of SR 50.

Type of Hiking
Hiking is level through pine flatlands and oak forests, along the edge of a swamp and on tree-lined dikes along the St. Johns River floodplain. The Reserve loop trails are good for day hikes. The trail in the Reserve is part of the Florida Recreational Trails System.

Parking
Park at Christmas RV Park on SR 50, at the youth camp in the Reserve and at Lone Cabbage fish camp at the bridge on SR 520. Day hikers in the Reserve should follow signs to ranch house parking.

Water
There is water at each terminus. Boil or treat surface water.

Conveniences
Supplies: Christmas
Mail: Christmas 32709
Motels: Cocoa and Titusville near Interstate 95
Public Campgrounds: none

Emergency
Orange County Sheriff: 407-657-2500
Manager: 407-568-5893

Precautions
Wear safety orange if you hike in the Reserve during special hunts (call the reserve for dates of special hunts). The Reserve is open from eight a.m. until sunset. You should carry a map and compass, because the intersecting trails and roads are confusing. Loop trails in the Reserve have white blazes; the rest of the blazes are orange.

Restrictions
Notify the Reserve office before hiking into the Reserve. Call 407-568-5893. The address is, Superintendent, 3365 Taylor Creek Rd., Christmas, FL 32709. Register at the office. Only backpack camping (you must have a reservation)

at designated sites is permitted in the Reserve. No conventional camping is permitted.

Description
Hikers may make an overnight hike or select one of several day hikes in the Reserve. On the north side of the Reserve, a trail leads to a virgin bald cypress stand in Jim Creek Swamp. Tosohatchee has a varied assortment of wildlife, including deer, turkey, osprey, and eagles and the dikes provide good vantage points. In the spring, the Reserve is colorful with wildflowers, including wild iris, which blooms in purple profusion in the woods, in the drainages and on the edge of the swamp.

There are two landmarks in the Reserve. One is a decrepit hunting shack called the "Hoot Owl Hilton." The other is the "Beehead ranchhouse," a large, well-preserved house made of native cypress and palm logs. A majestic virgin stand of pines is located just west of Beehead ranchhouse.

From 1930 until 1977, this area was used for the Tosohatchee Gun Club and was left untouched to encourage wildlife. The state acquired the reserve in 1977. The area contains at least 30 known Indian mounds.

Trail Data - Tosohatchee

Mileage S to N		Mileage N to S
16.9 ①	Northern terminus at SR 50 just east of Christmas RV Park. Cross fence near Alligator Farm. Trail follows woods road for 0.8 mile.	0.0
16.1	Cross north fence at border of Reserve.	0.8
16.0	Register in woods on trail. Trail blazed orange to north and white to south from old hunt cabin.	0.9
14.9	Cross Tosohatchee Creek near site of "Hoot Owl Hilton." Parking.	2.0
14.4	Junction of orange-blazed through-trail and white-blazed loop trail.	2.5
13.5	Cross powerline road and canal on vehicle bridge.	3.4
13.3	Cross Beehead Ranch Road.	3.6
12.2	Pass junction of old road and east-west cross trail	4.7
11.2	Cross Fish Hole Road.	5.7
11.0	Junction with 0.3 mile trail to Tiger Branch campsite. No water.	5.9
9.3	Cross Jim Creek on Fish Hole Road bridge.	7.6

7.8	Junction of orange-blazed trail to south and white-blazed loop trail.	9.1
7.7	Trail crosses Long Bluff Road.	9.2
7.3	Trail junction with Mud Lake canal. Follow north-south Mud Lake canal bank.	9.6
7.1	Cross spoil bank and canal on footbridge.	9.8
6.8	Route turns at east-west SR 528 canal overpass.	10.1
6.5	Trail passes edge of woods. Route follows east-west along north fence of highway.	10.4
6.0 ②	Cross under SR 528 (Beeline Highway) bridge. In high water periods, cross over on highway bridge.	10.9
5.9	Cross cut by wading. Trail follows cedar-lined dike through river floodplain.	11.0
5.3	Junction of spoil bank with dike and pipeline crossing.	11.6
3.8	Cross cuts in dike.	13.1
2.6	Trail on dike crosses cut on draw bridge. Follow north-south dike.	14.3
0.6	Trail turns at junction of floodplain dike and canal bank on SR 520. Route follows east-west canal bank along north side of SR 520.	16.3
0.0 ③	South terminus on SR 520 at edge of woods and the floodplain line.	16.9

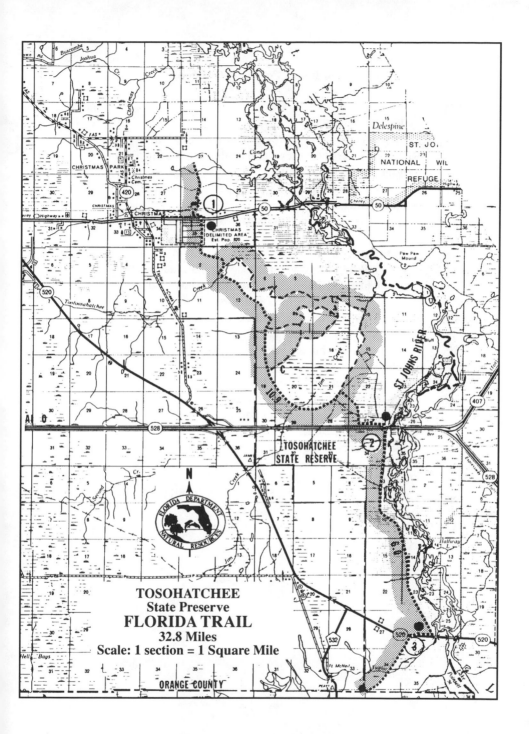

TOSOHATCHEE
State Preserve
FLORIDA TRAIL
32.8 Miles
Scale: 1 section = 1 Square Mile

Orange County

Trail Data - Tosohatchee Loop

Mileage Counterclockwise		Mileage Clockwise
15.9 ①	Loop trail (white blazes) junction with orange-blazed FT to north. Trail follows wood roads for 0.6 mile. Pass through woods for 1.0 mile.	0.0
14.3	Junction of woods trail with old jeep road. Trail follows old jeep road for 0.2 mile.	1.6
14.1	Trail junction with old jeep road. Pass through woods for 2.3 miles.	1.8
11.8	Trail in woods junction with trail on power line road. Trail follows power line road for 0.9 mile.	4.1
10.9	Trail on dike junction with trail on power line road.	5.0
9.7	Cross canal on water control structure.	6.2
8.7	Junction with 0.1 mile access trail to Whetrock Camp. No water.	7.2
6.6 ②	Loop trail (white blazes) junction with orange-blazed FT to south.	9.3
5.1	Trail crosses Jim Creek on Fish Hole Road bridge.	10.8
3.4	Junction with interior trail. Tiger Branch Camp is 0.3 mile on interior trail. Pit latrine.	12.5
3.2	Cross Fish Hole Road.	12.7
2.2	Trail crosses old road and junction with east-west cross trail.	13.7
1.6	Cross Beehead Ranch Road.	14.8
0.9	Cross power line road and canal on vehicle bridge. Trail passes through woods for 0.9 mile.	15.0
0.0	Loop trail (white blazes) junction with orange-blazed FT to north.	15.9

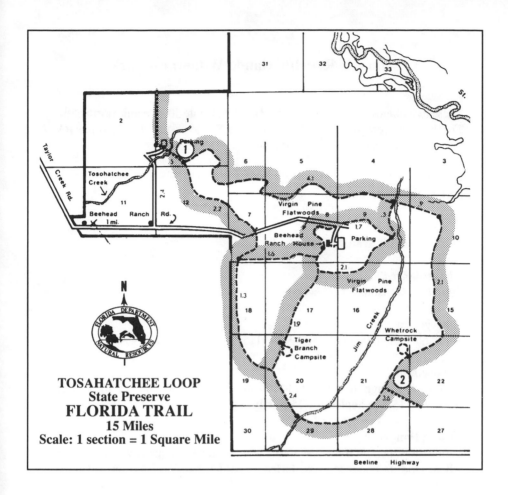

TOSAHATCHEE LOOP
State Preserve
FLORIDA TRAIL
15 Miles
Scale: 1 section = 1 Square Mile

Orange County

Seminole Ranch/Orlando Wilderness Park

Location
These two interesting areas are located north of Route 50, one mile north of the Tosohatchee Reserve. Enter from SR 50, 0.1 mile east of the Chrismas RV Park, or at the entrance to the parks on Wheeler Road.

Parking
Park at either entrance.

Water
Potable water is available at both entrances.

Conveniences
Supplies: Christmas, Longwood

Emergency
Seminole County Sheriff: 407-322-5115

Restrictions
Visitors must sign in at Seminole Ranch. Orlando Wilderness Park is open from May 15th to September 15th only.

Description
Seminole Ranch offers access to the edge of the St. Johns River floodplain, where wildlife abounds. The Orlando Wilderness Area is a birdwatcher's dream.

Trail Data - Seminole Ranch

Mileage Counterclockwise		Mileage Clockwise
	Wheeler Road entrance and parking area is 0.3 miles west of the trail head.	
6.2 ①	Begin/end Seminole Ranch loop.	0.0
5.5	Junction with Orlando Wilderness Park loop. Trail continues east/west.	0.7
4.7 ②	Junction with Orlando Wilderness Park loop. Trail turns south/west.	1.5
2.3	Junciton with 0.3 mile connector trail to/from SR 50 at spoil pond. Loop trail turns 90 degrees.	3.9
③	Southern terminus at SR 50 0.1 mile east of Christmas RV park.	

0.0 ①   Loop trail ends/begins.   6.2

Trail Data - Orlando Wilderness Park

4.4 ②   Begin/end loop north of Seminole Ranch loop.   0.0

3.3   Trail turns east/south.   1.1

1.1   Trail turns west/north. Intersects path to St. Johns   3.3
         River east of loop.

0.8   Trail intersects east edge of Seminole Ranch loop.   3.6

0.0 ②   Begin/end loop.   4.4

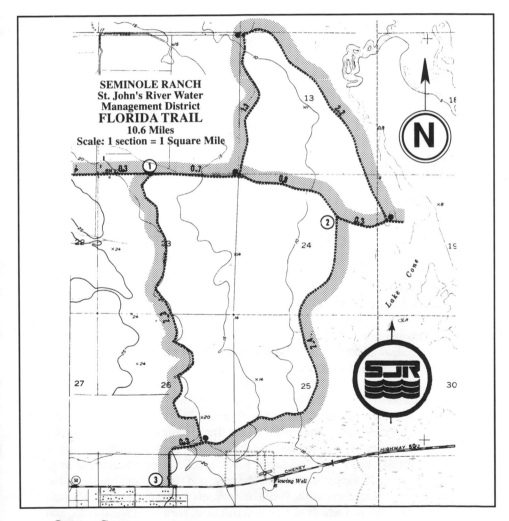

Orange County

Wekiwa Springs State Park

Location
Wekiwa Springs is north of Apopka, 3.0 miles east of CR 435 (via Welch Road) on Wekiwa Springs Road.

Type of Hiking
Overnight or day hikes are possible on this 13 mile white-blazed portion of the Florida trail, through jungle and forest terrain. Wading may be necessary in wet weather.

Parking
Park at the Sand Lake parking area. Get a permit from the park office.

Water
There is potable water at the main facilities in the park. Boil or treat spring water.

Conveniences
Supplies: Apopka
Motels: Apopka
Public Campgrounds: In the park

Emergency
Park; 407-884-2009
Park Manager: 407-884-2006
Orange County Sheriff: 407-648-3700

Precautions
Bears and raccoons are in the park. Hang food out of their reach.

Restrictions
Fires are allowed only in fire rings at designated campsites. The east campsite has limited space. Obtain a permit. The park closes at sundown.

Description
Wekiwa Springs State Park is a 6,400 acre preserve. Much of it still is as it was when the Timucuan Indians lived there. The primary feature is Wekiwa Springs, a crystal clear spring which is the source of the Wekiva River, part of which is designated a "Wild and Scenic River" in official records. Rock Springs is another spring, located just outside the park, and its beautiful run forms the north and east boundaries of the Park as it meanders to join the Wekiva. The trail passes through open woods of pine and palmetto, hardwood hammocks, and

wet, vine-tangled jungles. The trail makes several picturesque crossings of spring-fed streams. Animal life is abundant, including bear, deer, fox squirrels, wading birds, raccoons and alligators. Fishing is good. The park has a concession stand and the park entrance supplies brochures on the trail and on plants and wildlife. The park address is 1800 Wekiwa Circle, Apopka, FL 32703.

Trail Data - Wekiwa Springs State Park

Mileage Clockwise		Mileage Counterclockwise
10.2 ①	Terminus at Sand Lake parking area. Follow white-blazed trail 0.2 miles to main loop.	0.0
10.0	Junction with main loop trail. Trail passes along Sand Lake shore.	0.2
9.2	Junction with 1.0 mile blue-blazed cross trail. Trail follows old RR grade for 1.0 miles across Wekiva swamp.	1.0
8.2	North edge of swamp. Trail along Rock Springs Run for 0.8 mile.	2.0
7.4	Campsite at Springs Run Camp.	2.8
6.9	Trail crosses old RR grade.	3.3
5.7	Cross low area near Rock Springs Run.	4.5
4.0	Campsite at Live Oak Camp. Trail passes through highlands for 1.1 mile.	6.2
2.9	Cross Carpenter Branch at junction with 0.7 mile blue-blazed cross trail.	7.3
2.4	Pass north end of Lake Prevatt.	7.8
1.9	Trail crosses park road leading to group camp.	8.3
1.3	Trail crosses main park road.	8.9
1.2	Junction with blue-blazed 0.9 mile trail to park HQ.	9.0
0.4	Junction with yellow-blazed 0.9 mile cross trail. Trail through woods for 0.2 mile.	9.8
0.2	Junction with main loop trail. Follow white-blazed trail 0.2 miles to main loop.	10.0
0.0	Terminus at Sand Lake parking area.	10.2

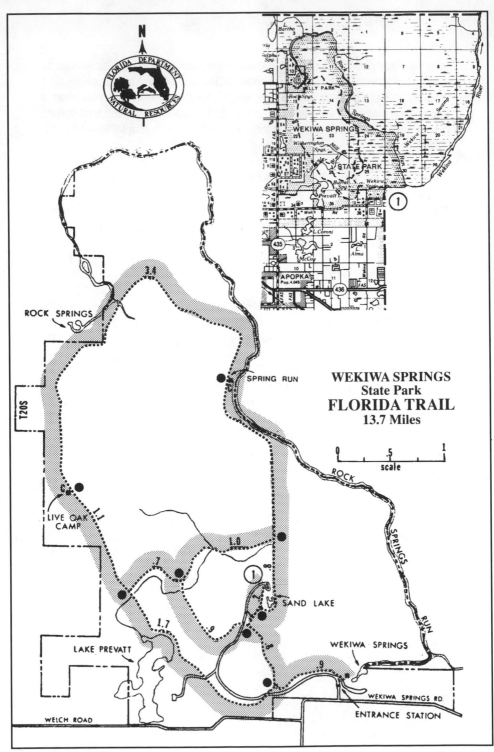

N

FLORIDA DEPARTMENT
NATURAL RESOURCES

ROCK SPRINGS

T20S

SPRING RUN

WEKIWA SPRINGS
State Park
FLORIDA TRAIL
13.7 Miles

0   .5   1
scale

ROCK

SPRINGS

3.4

LIVE OAK
CAMP

1.1

1.0

.7

.8

.9

①

1.7

.9

SAND LAKE

WEKIWA SPRINGS

LAKE PREVATT

RUN

WEKIWA SPRINGS RD.

WELCH ROAD

ENTRANCE STATION

Orange County

Lake Arbuckle National Recreational Trail

Location
The trail is on SR 64, about ten miles east of the US 27 intersection in Avon Park. The trail is in the Avon Park bombing range, which includes the Avon Park Air Force Base. Enter only through the Air Force gate on SR 64 at the south end of Lake Arbuckle.

Type of Hiking
Both overnight and day hikes may be made through pine palmetto flatlands, oak and hardwood forests and river floodplains. The trail is mostly dry.

Parking
Park at Willingham campsite (as shown on map).

Water
There is potable water at the Air Force Headquarters, at Willingham and at halfway campsites. Boil or treat all other water.

Conveniences
Supplies: At Avon Park and at store two miles from the AF gate.
Mail: Avon Park 33825
Motels: Avon Park
Public Campgrounds: Highlands Hammock State Park, Sebring

Emergency
USAF Security Police: 813-452-4195
USAF Natural Resources Office: 813-453-4119
Polk County Sheriff: 813-533-0444

Precautions
Call USAF (813-452-4119) before hiking for information about current restrictions and hunting seasons. *Do not touch any devices resembling munitions.* This trail is near an active bombing area. Do not leave the trail. *The U.S. Government assumes no liability for injuries to persons hiking this trail!*

Restrictions
Hike only with permission of USAF (813-452-4195). *Check in and out* with Security Police at Building 425. The trail is closed to hikers during general hunting season. Build campfires only at designated campsites and leave no trace of fire.

Description

This trail goes through the NW corner of the Avon Park Wildlife Management Area, northwest of the bombing range. The trail passes through typical central Florida terrain, a mixture of pine palmetto flatland, oak and hardwood hammock, commercial pine plantations and marshy floodplain. Wildlife, especially waterfowl, is abundant. You may see osprey, sandhill cranes, eagles and the distinctively marked Audubon's caracara. The trail passes Fort Arbuckle, a historic site. Since the land is leased to ranchers, you will encounter cattle. The Lake Arbuckle Trail has been designated part of the National Recreational Trail System.

Trail Data - Lake Arbuckle Trail

Mileage Counterclockwise		Mileage Clockwise
15.0 ①	Terminus at Willingham Campsite; toilet, water, parking.	0.0
14.5	Cross stream on bridge.	0.5
14.4	Cross Willingham Grade.	0.6
14.3	Trail goes through a pass-through at locked gate.	0.7
13.6	Pass site of old Ft. Arbuckle.	1.4
12.0	Trail crosses Frostproof Road.	3.0
11.3	Trail passes through pine plantation.	3.7
9.8	Climb over locked gate at hinge post end.	5.2
8.8	Trail junction with Degogne Grade. Trail follows Degogne Grade for 1.0 mile.	6.2
7.8	Trail and Degogne Grade junction.	7.2
6.2	Pass cattle-dipping vat.	8.8
6.0	Campsite, well. Trail follows old forest roads for 3.2 miles.	9.0
2.8	Cross Billig Grade. Trail passes through pine plantation.	12.0
0.0	Terminus at Willingham Campsite.	15.0

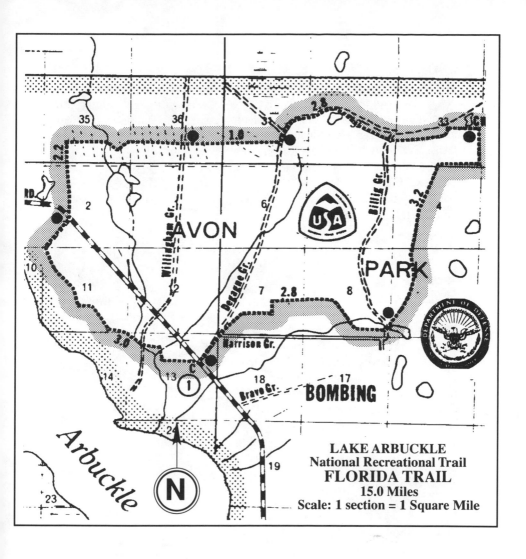

LAKE ARBUCKLE
National Recreational Trail
FLORIDA TRAIL
15.0 Miles
Scale: 1 section = 1 Square Mile

Polk County

Lake Kissimmee State Park

Location
Lake Kissimmee State Park is 14 miles NE of the City of Lake Wales. Signs on SR 60 mark the turn onto the county road leading to the park.

Type of Hiking
This level trail affords beautiful lakefront views. A campsite is available for an overnight hike.

Parking
Park between the two trail loops (see map).

Water
There is potable water at the main park facilities. Boil or treat all surface water.

Conveniences
Supplies: Lake Wales and along SR 60
Mail: Lake Wales 33853
Motels: Lake Wales
Public Campground: Lake Kissimmee State Park

Emergency
Polk County Sheriff: 813-533-0444
Park Superintendent: 813-696-1112

Precautions
Gates are open between eight a.m. and sunset. The main trail is blazed white. Connecting trails are blazed blue.

Restrictions
Hikers must register with a ranger for use of the primitive campsites. Small fires are permitted only at designated backpacking campsites. No alcohol is permitted. Swimming is not permitted. *Pets must be leashed.* No firearms, bows or crossbows are permitted.

Description:
This trail has been officially designated as a part of the Florida Recreational Trails System. Lake Kissimmee State Park is a 5,030-acre preserve near three lakes: Kissimmee, Tiger and Rosalie. The area is geologically known as the Osceola Plain. The trail traverses lakeshore floodplain prairies, marshes, pine flatwoods, and live oak hammocks. Buster Island is a dry, sandy area of

elevated ground with a circular border of hardwood hammock. Gobbler Ridge was built up by the Lake Kissimmee storm waves and is now covered by large live oaks. Many species live in this park, including deer, eagles, sandhill cranes, turkeys and bobcats. Florida panthers once lived in this area, but there are probably none left here now. The developed area of the park is also worth visiting. An observation platform provides a spectacular view of Lake Kissimmee. The Park also features a reconstructed 1876 cow camp complete with scrub cows, and a "cow hunter." The park address is Rt.4, Box 243, Lake Wales, FL 33853.

Trail Data - Lake Kissimmee State Park

Mileage Clockwise		Mileage Counterclockwise
	North Loop	
5.6	Junction of north loop trail and access trail.	0.0
5.5	Trail crosses park road.	0.1
5.1	Junction with blue-blazed Gobbler Ridge trail.	0.5
4.6	Trail crosses park road.	1.0
3.8	Trail crosses park road.	1.8
2.7	Trail passes turpentine workers' cemetery (circa 1912).	2.9
2.2	Trail crosses park road.	3.4
1.4	Trail passes campsite.	4.2
0.0	Junction of north loop trail and access trail.	5.6

① Terminus at parking area. Look for trail sign at west edge of parking area. 0.5 mile trails (blue blazed) to loops. Trail to Buster Island Loop crosses Zipprer Canal Bridge.

Buster Island Loop

0.0	Junction of Buster Island loop trail and access trail. Trail passes through large pangola grass field.	5.9
0.8	Trail crosses old barbed wire fence.	5.1
1.6	Trail passes through oak hammock.	4.3
2.5	Trail junction with Buster Island campsite. Camping permitted within 50 paces of sign. Trail passes through woods.	3.4
5.9	Junction of Buster Island loop trail and access trail.	0.0

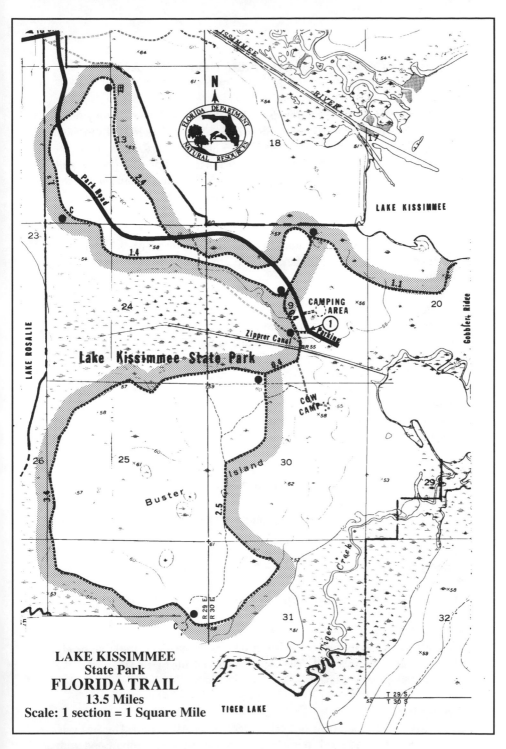

LAKE KISSIMMEE
State Park
FLORIDA TRAIL
13.5 Miles
Scale: 1 section = 1 Square Mile

Polk County

Little Manatee River State Recreation Area

Location
The trail borders US 301, seven miles north of Parrish (Manatee County), or approximately five miles south of SR 674/Sun City Center (Hillsborough County). Directional signs are located on US 301 both north and south of the park. Hikers must sign in at the entrance ranger station and get the gate combination for the hiking parking area. From I-75, take the Sun City Center exit, then drive east on SR 674 to US 301 south.

Type of Hiking
The trail is flat and mostly dry along the river bank and through oak hammocks, sand pine land and palmetto uplands. The 6.2 mile trail has 19 bridges and two boardwalks.

Parking
The hiking trail parking area is three miles north of the park entrance and a fourth of a mile north of the US 301 bridge over the Little Manatee River. Park personnel will direct you specifically; you must get the lock combination from a ranger to get into the lot.

Water
There is no potable water on the hiking trail or at the primitive campground, but it is available at the park headquarters.

Conveniences
Supplies: Chain food store at Sun City Center
Motels: Sun City Center
Public Campground: LMRSRA has numerous campsites. Hookups available. Daily fee.

Emergency
LMRSRA: 813-634-4781
Hillsborough County Sheriff Dept: 911

Precautions
The park opens at eight a.m. and closes at sunset. On the hiking trail, camp only at the primitive campground. The hiking trail has white blazes; the trail to the campground has blue blazes.

Description
LMRSRA is a new facility in the DNR system. The park is divided by the Little Manatee River. The south portion features a developed campground with

shower/toilet facilities, a canoe launch and a horse trail. The north portion is undeveloped except for the hiking trail and the primitive campground. The hiking trail gate described above is the only access to the north portion. Turkey, deer, bobcats, foxes and a colony of scrub jays live in the north portion. Botany enthusiasts will enjoy identifying hickory, various types of bay, pennyroyal, holly and wild azalea along the trail.

Trail Data - Little Manatee River State Recreation Area

Mileage Counterclockwise			Mileage Clockwise
		Trail begins 0.1 mile from the parking area	
6.2	(1)	Trailhead.	0.0
4.6		Cypress Creek Bridge.	1.6
2.3	(2)	Junction with 0.2-mile blue-blazed trail to primitive campground.	3.9
1.3		Cypress Creek Bridge.	4.9
0.0		Junction of access trail and loop.	6.2

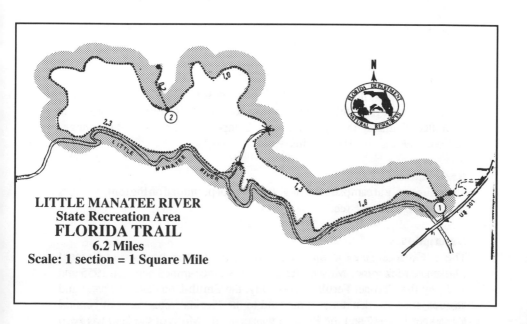

LITTLE MANATEE RIVER
State Recreation Area
FLORIDA TRAIL
6.2 Miles
Scale: 1 section = 1 Square Mile

Hillsborough County

Tenoroc Reserve

Location
The trail is located on SR 33A, 3.5 miles north of U.S. 92, or 2.5 miles south of I-4 in the Tenoroc Reserve.

Type of Hiking
The trail is mostly flat and dry and runs over reclaimed mining property covered with palmetto and oak hammocks.

Parking
Park at the family picnic grounds parking lot.

Water
Potable water is available in the restroom building at the west end of the parking lot.

Conveniences
Supplies: Lakeland. U.S. 92 and SR 33
Mail: Lakeland 33801
Motels: Lakeland
Public camprounds: Saddle Creek Park (Polk County) 813-665-2283

Emergencies
Polk County Sheriff: 813-533-0344

Precautions
The park is open Monday through Wednesday from eight a.m. to five p.m.; Thursday through Sunday from sunrise to sunset. Overnight camping is permitted Thursday through Saturday. Campers must register at the ranger station. The trail is blazed white.

Restrictions
Campfires only at campsite fire ring. Pets are not permitted on the trail. Visitors must pay an entrance fee.

Description
The 6,000-acre Tenoroc State Reserve is the former site of the Coronet Phosphate rock mine. Most of the land was surface-mined between 1955 and 1977 by the Coronet Fertilizer company, the Smith-Douglass company and Borden, Inc. Borden donated the land to the Florida Department of Natural Resources in 1982 and the Reserve was created. Much of the land has been reclaimed, and reclamation continues. The nearly 1,000 acres of lakes created

by the mining are managed for fishing by the Florida Department of Natural Resources and by the Florida Game and Fresh Water Fish Commission.

The terrain along the Tenoroc trail is unlike that in any other section of the Florida Trail System. Much of the trail runs through open areas. Many birds, mostly ospreys and water birds, live in the area. The campsite, nestled in an oak hammock, is especially pleasant.

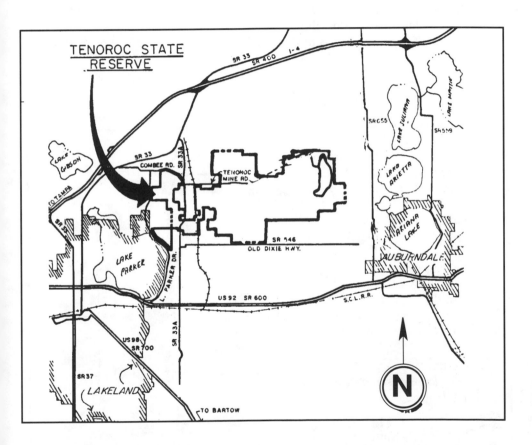

Polk County

Trail Data - Tenoroc Reserve

Mileage Clockwise			Mileage Counterclockwise
0.0	①	Terminus at access road to picnic area. Look for sign on east side of road. Trail through a field, a gate, then on an abandoned road along open water and up onto a dam top. Blazes mostly on posts.	5.9
1.5	②	Junction of loop trail. Trail mostly on little-used roads through undisturbed land.	4.5
2.9	③	Campsite 50 yards east of trail. Trail on graded dam tops.	3.0
4.4		Junction of loop trail.	1.5
5.9		Terminus at access road to picnic area.	0.0

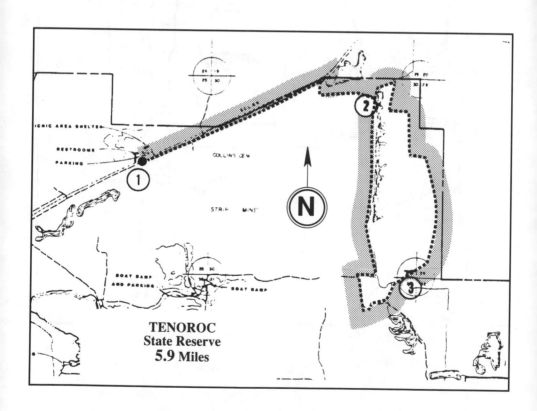

TENOROC
State Reserve
5.9 Miles

Polk County

Hillsborough River State Park

Location
Hillsborough River State Park is on US 301, six miles south of Zephyr Hills and nine miles north of Thonotosassa.

Type of Hiking
The terrain is flat, and usually dry along the river bank. Sometimes it is wet in hammocks and along creeks.

Parking
Park at parking areas near the walkway to the Park concession building.

Water
There is no water at the campsite. Carry four quarts for an overnight trip.

Conveniences
Supplies: 2.5 miles south on US 301 and at Park concession building (limited).
Mail: Thonotosassa 33592
Motels: Temple Terrace, Zephyrhills
Public Campgrounds: in Park.

Emergency
Hillsborough County Sheriff: 813-247-6411
Park Manager: 813-986-1020

Precautions
The park opens at eight a.m. and closes at sunset. The main loop trail is blazed white. Side trails are blazed blue.

Restrictions
Fees are charged for entrance to the park and for backpack camping. Backpack camping is permitted only at the established trail campsite. There is a limit of 12 persons per night at the trail campsite. Campfires are allowed only in fire circle at the trail campsite.

Description
Constructed by the Civilian Conservation Corps in 1936, Hillsborough River State Park is one of the oldest Florida state parks. The river through the park is noted for its rapids and surrounding hammock country. Visitors may find wild turkeys, pileated woodpeckers, barred owls, red shouldered hawks, otters, and deer. Canoes and paddle boats are available, and there is a launch site for

private canoes. To reach the hiking trail head, cross over the bridge near the concession building to the north side of the river on the Baynard nature trail. Walk north on the Baynard for 100 yards and find the hiking trail start point sign on the left.

Trail Data - Hillsborough River State Park

Mileage S to N		Mileage N to S
	Cross from parking area to north side of Hillsborough River on bridge. Find access trail sign on nature trail. Follow 0.1 mile access trail to junction with main loop trail.	
3.2	Junction of main loop trail and 0.1 mile access trail. Trail passes through rich hammock.	0.0
2.2	Junction of main loop trail and 0.1 mile blue-blazed trail to campsite in oak and pine woods. No water (C). Trail passes through rich hammock.	1.0
1.4	Arrive/leave riverside. Trail follows bank of Hillsborough River.	1.8
0.0	Junction of main loop trail and 0.1 mile access trail.	3.2

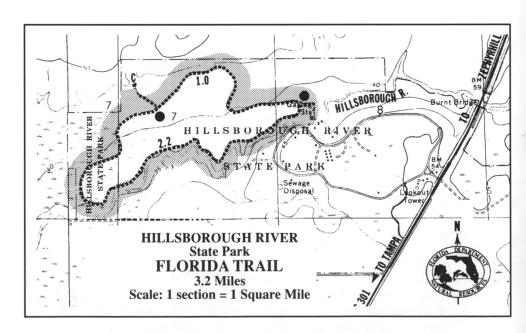

HILLSBOROUGH RIVER
State Park
FLORIDA TRAIL
3.2 Miles
Scale: 1 section = 1 Square Mile

Hillsborough County

Green Swamp

Location
The Green Swamp area is 20 miles north of Lakeland in the Southwest Florida Water Management District's Green Swamp Flood Detention Area. The south terminus is on Rock Ridge Road, ten miles northeast of US 98 or six miles west of SR 33 via Green Pond or Poyner Road. The north terminus is at Meg's Hole, 0.8 mile from the Richloam loop trail, and 0.5 mile south of Lacoochee-Clay Sink Road.

Type of Hiking
Hikers may use the Green Swamp loop trail for both overnight and day hiking. The trail wanders through pine flatwoods, tree farms, hardwood forests, and the floodplain of the Withlacoochee River. The northern portion of the through-trail in Devil's Creek Swamp is an aquifer recharge area and water levels can be high during wet seasons; you may have to wade.

Parking
Park at the Rock Ridge gate at the south terminus. At the north terminus, park at the junction of Clay Sink Road and Old Highway 50.

Water
There is no potable water on the trail. Boil or treat ground water.

Conveniences
Supplies: Lakeland, Polk City, Dade City, Zephyrhills, and SR33
Mail: Polk City 33868
Motels: In above locations
Public Campgrounds: Saddle Creek Park (Polk County)

Emergencies
Polk County Sheriff: 813-533-0344
Southwest Fla. Water Management District: 904-796-7211
Sumter County Sheriff: 904-793-0222

Precautions
Use caution during general hunting season.

Restrictions
The trail is closed to hikers during the first nine days of general hunting season, and during Thanksgiving, Christmas and New Years holidays.
Camp only in designated sites. Fires are permitted only in fire rings. Fires are not permitted during fire bans and during obvious dry conditions.

Description

The Green Swamp, 870 square miles of land in Polk, Lake, Sumter, Hernando, and Pasco counties, contains the headwaters of the Withlacoochee, Hillsborough, Oklawaha, and Peace Rivers. The area contains pine flatwoods, hardwood forests, cypress heads, swamps and river floodplains. A part of the trail follows an old logging railroad grade within the Withlacoochee River floodplain. Wildlife commonly seen are deer, wild hogs, turkeys, alligators and a great variety of birds. This environment is a classic example of an aquifer recharge area.

Trail Data - Green Swamp Loop

Mileage Counterclockwise			Mileage Clockwise
8.4	(2)	Junction of loop trail & main grade road.	0.0
8.3		Junction of trail with SE end of day loop trail. Trail follows old RR grade.	0.1
7.5	(3)	Trail junction with side trail to scenic overlook.	0.9
7.1		Junction of trail (on woods road) and NW end of day loop trail. Trail follows woods road.	1.3
6.2		Pass 0.3 mile side trail to Mott Hammock campsite. No water. Trail follows woods road for 0.3 mile. Trail passes through pine flatwoods for 0.7 mile.	2.2
5.2		Junction with main through-trail to/from Richloam (15.4 miles).	3.2
5.1		Pass Stewart Place at main grade road.	3.3
4.8		Cross Powder Grade road. Trail passes through pine flatwoods and tree farm.	3.6
3.9		Pass line between old pines and open area of smaller pines. Trail passes through open area for 1.0 mile. Trail goes through tree farm and woods for 1.2 miles.	4.5
1.7		Junction with woods road.	6.7
1.5		Pass Tillman Hammock campsite. No water. Trail follows woods road.	6.9
1.2		Junction with woods road.	7.2
1.0		Junction with old RR grade.	7.4
0.5		Trail crosses footbridge.	7.9
0.0	(2)	Junction of loop trail and main grade road.	8.4

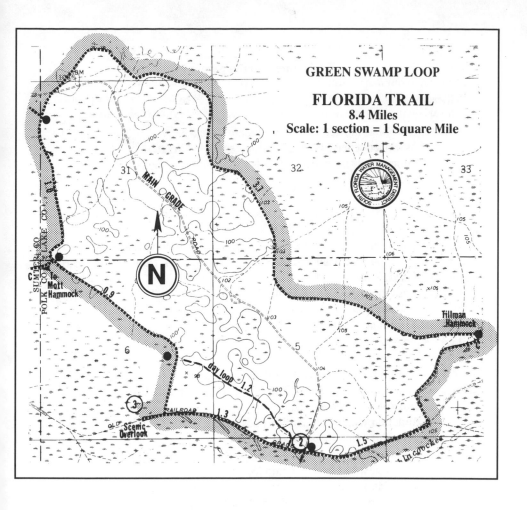

GREEN SWAMP LOOP

FLORIDA TRAIL
8.4 Miles
Scale: 1 section = 1 Square Mile

Lake County

Trail Data - Green Swamp

Mileage S to N		Mileage N to S
19.3 ⑤	Terminus at Meg's Hole, Richloam Tract, Withlacoochee SF. Trail follows east-west roads.	0.0
17.7	Junction with east-west woods road. Trail on South Loop Road.	1.6
17.1	Cross SR 471.	2.2
17.0	Junction with north-south woods road. Trail on north-south woods road.	2.3
16.4	Junction with south loop road. Trail on south loop road.	2.9
13.7	Junction with Tanic Grade Road. Trail follows Tanic Grade Road.	5.6
13.5 ④	Pass through Green Swamp-Richloam gate. Trail follows Tanic Grade Road.	5.8
12.8	Trail junction with Tanic Grade Road.	6.5
12.4	Pass campsite north of trail. Trail mostly east-west on woods road.	6.9
10.9	Trail junction with east-west woods road.	8.4
9.2	Cross culvert on Three Run Grade Road. Trail follows mostly N-S woods road.	10.1
7.2	Junction with north-south woods road.	12.1
6.6	Pass through cypress head.	12.7
6.0	Cross main grade road.	13.3
5.7	Junction with Green Swamp loop trail (see loop trail map/data). Trail passes through pine flatwoods for 0.7 mile. Trail follows woods road for 0.3 mile.	13.6
4.7	Pass 0.3 mile side trail to Mott Hammock campsite. No water. Trail follows woods road.	14.6
3.8	Junction of trail (on woods road) and NW end of day loop trail.	15.5
3.4 ③	Trail junction with side trail to scenic overlook. Trail follows old RR grade.	15.9
2.6	Junction of trail with SE end of day loop trail.	16.7
2.5	Trail junction with main grade road.	16.8
②	Trail crosses Withlacoochee River on main grade.	
2.2	Trail on and off main grade road for 1.5 miles. Pass Grass Creek.	17.1
0.7	Pass Game & Fish Commission gate. Register. Trail on main grade road for 0.2 mile. Trail on RR grade. Pass hunter campsite.	18.6
0.0 ①	Terminus at Rock Ridge Road gate.	19.3

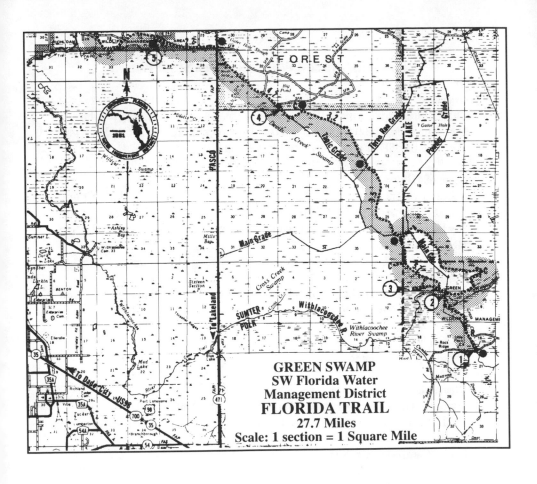

GREEN SWAMP
SW Florida Water
Management District
FLORIDA TRAIL
27.7 Miles
Scale: 1 section = 1 Square Mile

Hernando, Lake, Pasco, Polk, Sumter Counties

Richloam Tract - Withlacoochee State Forest

Location
The Richloam tract is in the Withlacoochee State Forest, 10 miles north of Dade City. The access point is at the junction of Clay Sink Road and Old Highway 50, 0.4 miles SE of SR 50 on Clay Sink Road.

Type of Hiking
The trail offers mostly dry hiking, with some shallow wading during rainy seasons. The perimeter trail offers a 25 mile overnight hike. Several different day hikes can be made by crossing the perimeter on graded roads to make 5 to 10 mile loops.

Parking
Park at the junction of Clay Sink Road and Old Highway 50 at the fire tower. Do not block the driveway.

Water
There is potable water at the Richloam Tower. Boil or treat all surface water.

Conveniences
Supplies: Dade City and at the intersection of SR50 and SR301.
Mail: Dade City 33525, Brooksville 33512
Motels: Dade City and Brooksville
Public Campgrounds: Silver Lake Recreation Area (Croom)

Emergency
Hernando County Sheriff: 904-796-3541
Pasco County Sheriff: 813-847-5878
Forest Headquarters (Brooksville): 904-796-5650

Precautions
Hiking is not advised during general hunting season.

Restrictions
The trail is closed to hikers during the first nine days of general hunting season, and during Thanksgiving, Christmas and New Years holidays. Camping is permitted only within zones marked with white bands on trees. Cooking fires are allowed only in camping zones. No bonfires are permitted. Do not build a fire if a Class 5 fire day sign is posted, or during dry conditions.

Description

The Richloam trail offers a wide variety of plant and animal life. The trail passes through cypress bayheads, pine-palmetto flatlands, hardwood hammocks and open pine prairies. The trail borders the Withlacoochee River in the southwest and the Little Withlacoochee River in the northern section, and crosses numerous streams which drain the tract. As in the other Withlacoochee tracts, wildflowers are abundant from March until November. Eagles, deer, turkeys, bluebirds and several other native Florida animals inhabit the Richloam tract. Fishing is good here. This loop trail is part of the West Central Florida Trail loop system and connects to the Green Swamp loop trail system. A brochure is available from Forest Supervisor's Office, Withlacoochee State Forest, 15023 Broad St., Brooksville, FL 33512.

Trail Data - Richloam

Mileage Counterclockwise		Mileage Clockwise
25.3	Terminus at Richloam Tower. Water, Register.	0.0
25.1 (1)	Junction of main loop and access trail.	0.2
24.3	Trail follows parallel to SR 50, south side.	1.0
23.9	Cross SR 50.	1.4
22.4	Trail crosses McKinney Sink Road	2.9
20.8	Pass west side of Boat Pond.	4.5
20.3	Reach Island Prairie Pond.	5.0
20.1 (2)	Cross McKinney Sink Road.	5.2
19.0 (3)	Trail passes through Little River Camp Zone. Camp within white bands. Treat water.	6.3
17.1	Trail crosses Pole Bridge Road.	8.2
14.6 (4)	Trail crosses SR 50.	10.7
14.1	Cross old SR 50. Follow old SR 50 for 0.1 mile. Watch blazes.	11.2
11.9	Camp zone 100 yds. west on blue blazed trail.	13.4
10.5 (5)	Cross graded Riverland Road	14.8
9.0	Trail crosses Clay Sink Road. Richloam Tower. Pass through Jesse Hammock.	16.3
8.1	Trail crosses School Bus Road.	17.2
7.2	Cross Lacoochee Road.	18.1
7.0 (6)	Junction with trail to Green Swamp via Megs Hole. Camping zone, latrine.	18.3
4.4	Cross fence on stepover.	20.9
4.2 (7)	Junction with blue-blazed side trail through camp zone for high river level use.	21.1
3.3	Junction with blue-blazed trail to Big River camp.	22.0

	zone. Camp within white bands. High water trail.	
2.8 ⑧	Cross Lacoochee Road.	22.5
2.3	Cross creek on log bridge.	23.0
1.6	Follows high graded road for 0.1 mile (old R.R. grade).	23.7
1.5	Trail follows jeep road. Crosses grade diagonally at cattle guard.	23.8
0.2	Junction of main loop and blue-blazed access trail.	25.1
0.0	Terminus at Richloam Tower. Water. Register.	25.3

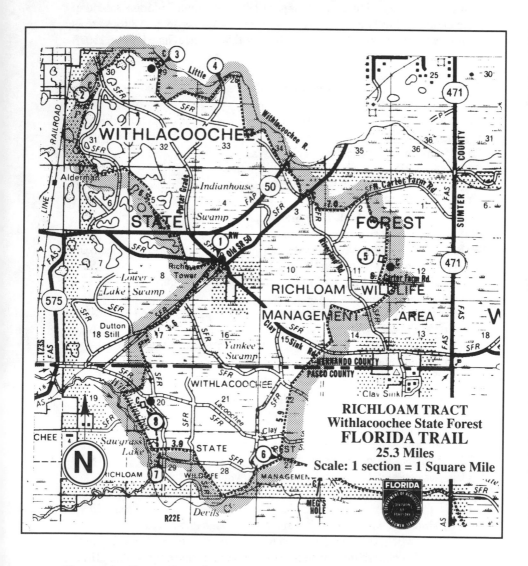

RICHLOAM TRACT
Withlacoochee State Forest
FLORIDA TRAIL
25.3 Miles
Scale: 1 section = 1 Square Mile

Hernando, Pasco Counties

Croom Tract - Withlacoochee State Forest

Location
The Croom tract is in the center tract of Withlacoochee State Forest east of Brooksville. Enter at the Silver Lake recreation area. Proceed four miles north on the road from the intersection with US 98 (SR 50), one mile east of the I-75 overpass at the Brooksville-Orlando exit. Look for the large FT sign near the boat ramp at the north end of Silver Lake recreation area near the Interstate 75 bridge over the Withlacoochee River. The Hog Island Trail access at the north end is at Hog Island recreation area off SR 476 and CR 635 east of No-bleton, and at the south end off of SR 478 via state forest roads to River Junction recreation area.

Type of Hiking
The Croom tract affords dry, all weather hiking on slightly hilly terrain. There is an overnight 20 mile hike on the perimeter, or you may plan day hikes on any of three loops.

Parking
Park at Silver Lake recreation area, or where the trail crosses Forest Road T6 (Tucker Hill Tower).

Water
Find water at Silver Lake recreation area, and Tucker Hill tower. Boil or treat all other water.

Conveniences
Supplies: Brooksville
Mail: Brooksville 33512
Motels: Brooksville
Public Campgrounds: Silver Lake, River Junction, and Hog
        Island Recreation Areas

Emergency
Forest Headquarters: 904-796-5650
Hernando County Sheriff: 904-583-3541

Precautions
Camping zones, marked by white banded trees, are shown on the map.

Restrictions
The trail is closed to hikers during general hunting season. Camping and campfires are permitted only at authorized camping zones; only cooking fires are permitted. Do not build fires when "Class five" fire danger signs are posted.

Description

The terrain is similar to that in the Citrus tract of the Withlacoochee State Forest. The trail passes through sandhill scrub, oak thickets and stands of pine and past creek bottoms and cypress ponds. Hiking the hilly northern section with a heavy pack will quickly provide conditioning for mountain trail hiking. There are two deep ravines on the Croom Trail, one close to the Tucker Hill Tower entrance and another on C-Loop. The blue-blazed loop to Silver Lake is really two trails. Follow the river trail when water is low, and use the high trail after prolonged rainy periods. There is swimming at Silver Lake. The popular Hog Island Trail skirts the river and passes through an entire range of ecosystems. Brochure is available from Forest Supervisor's Office, Withlacoochee State Forest, 15023 Broad St., Brooksville, FL 33512.

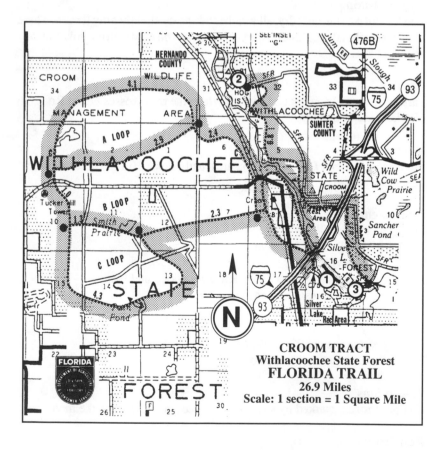

CROOM TRACT
Withlacoochee State Forest
FLORIDA TRAIL
26.9 Miles
Scale: 1 section = 1 Square Mile

Hernando County

Trail Data- Croom

Mileage Clockwise		Mileage Counterclockwise
20.1 ①	Terminus at Silver Lake recreation area. Restrooms, water, parking. Look for FT trail sign near boat ramp. Follow blue blazes under I-75 bridge .	0.0
20.0	Junction highland and lowland trails. Use 1.3 mile highland trail during floods. Lowland trail passes along rivers.	0.1
18.1	Trail crosses paved Croom Road and old RR bed.	2.0
17.6	Junction Highland and Lowland access trails.	2.5
17.1	Junction main "B" loop and Silver Lake Access trails.	3.0
16.6	Cross paved Croom Road (T6).	3.5
16.3	Camping zone.	3.8
14.7	Junction "A-B" blue-blazed 2.9 mile cross trail. Trail ascends and descends many hills.	5.4
12.7	Trail passes Lunch Stop Hill.	7.4
10.7	Camping Zone.	9.4
10.6	Junction "A-B" blue blazed 2.9 mile cross trail.	9.5
10.3	Cross Croom Road (T6). Register, water, parking.	9.8
9.6	Junction "B-C" blue blazed 1.3 mile cross trail.	10.5
8.4	Cross abandoned railroad grade.	11.7
7.2	Trail passes Twin Pond.	12.9
5.8	Cross abandoned railroad grade.	14.3
5.3	Junction "B-C" blue blazed 1.3 mile cross trail.	14.8
3.0	Junction main "B" loop and Silver Lake access trails.	17.1
2.5	Junction Highland and Lowland access trails.	17.6
2.0	Cross paved Croom Road and old RR bed.	18.1
0.1	Junction highland and lowland trails. Use 1.3 mile highland trail during floods. Lowland trail passes along rivers	20.0
0.0	Terminus at Silver Lake recreation area.	20.1

Hog Island Trail

6.8 ②	Terminus at Hog Island campground. Restrooms, water, parking.	0.0
6.2	Trail passes Sawdust Pond.	0.6
3.9	Pass along river bend.	2.9
2.6	Pass Iron Bridge recreation area.	4.2
1.6	Trail passes under I-75.	5.2
0.0 ③	Terminus at River Junction Campground. Restrooms, water, parking.	6.8

Citrus Tract - Withlacoochee State Forest

Location
This 11,000 acre tract is in the Withlacoochee State Forest south of SR 44, and just southwest of Inverness. Enter at Holder Mine recreation area via Road 10 from SR 581, 2 1/2 miles south of SR 44, or at Mutual Mine recreation area via Road 16 from SR 581, 5 1/4 miles south of SR 44.

Type of Hiking
Citrus tract is a dry, all-weather trail on alternately flat and hilly terrain. You may plan day hikes on loop trails and overnight hikes of up to 40 miles on the perimeter trail.

Parking
Park at Holder Mine and Mutual Mine recreation areas.

Water
Water is available at the recreation areas. Boil, filter or treat all surface water.

Conveniences
Supplies: Inverness.
Mail: Inverness 32650
Motels: Inverness
Public Campgrounds: Mine Recreation Areas

Emergency
Hernando County Sheriff: 904-583-3541
Forest Headquarters: 904-796-5650

Precautions
Use caution when exploring in mine dumps or sink holes. Hiking is not advised during general hunting season. Avoid Citrus horse trail, which is blazed with blue bands around the trees.

Restrictions
The trail is closed to hikers during the first nine days of general hunting season. Camping and campfires are permitted only within the established zones (the trees are marked with white bands). Only cooking fires are permitted. Do not build bonfires. No fires are permitted when Fire Danger Alert signs read Class five.

Description
This trail passes through sandhill scrub, oak thickets, stands of sand pine and long leaf pine and hardwood forests. Limestone sink holes are a distinguishing feature. Citrus is one of the few places where the large, colorful fox squirrel can be seen in abundance. Like Richloam, Citrus offers hilly terrain, and two days in Citrus with a heavy pack is great conditioning for mountain trail trips. Sink holes are good places to look for fossils and relics. The Citrus area, like most other state forest tracts is laced with unimproved roads. This road network, and the interconnecting trail links, make it possible to plan a variety of hikes.

Trail Data - Citrus

S to N		N to S
40.6	Main north access at west side of Holder Mine Recreation Area. Camping, water, register. Look for FT sign. Trail follows blue blazes past sawdust pile.	0.0
39.7	Junction of main "A" loop and access trail from Holder Mine area.	0.9
37.7	Trail crosses limestone road T6.	2.9
37.5 ①	Top of hill at Bull Sink.	3.1
35.4	Junction with "A" - "B" blue-blazed 1.6 mile cross trail.	5.2
33.6	Trail passes cistern.	7.0
28.4	Junction with 0.6 mile side trail to Perryman Place. Camping zone, water and latrine.	12.2
25.9	Junction with "B" - "C" blue-blazed 1.6 mile cross trail.	14.7
23.9	Camping zone. Junction with Road 15.	16.7
21.3	Junction with "C" - "D" blue-blazed 1.8 mile cross trail.	19.3
17.4	Trail passes Lizzie Hart sink.	23.2
15.7	Trail crosses SR 480.	24.9
14.6	Camping zone. Junction with Road 13.	26.0
12.6	Trail crosses SR 480.	28.0
9.2	Junction with "C" - "D" blue-blazed 1.8 mile cross trail.	31.4
8.4	Trail crosses old R.R. bed.	32.2
7.8	Junction of main "C" loop and 1.5 mile access trail from Mutual Mine recreation area. Camping, water, register. At Mutual Mine find F.T. sign. Trail starts 100 ft. north of register at fence stile.	32.8
7.2	Cross old railroad bed.	33.4
4.7	Trail passes animal watering tank.	35.9
3.2	Junction with "B" - "C" blue-blazed 1.6 mile cross trail.	37.4
1.7	Junction with "A" - "B" blue-blazed 1.6 mile cross trail.	38.9
0.9	Junction of main "A" loop and access trail.	39.7
0.0	Main north access at Holder Mine, see top of page.	40.6

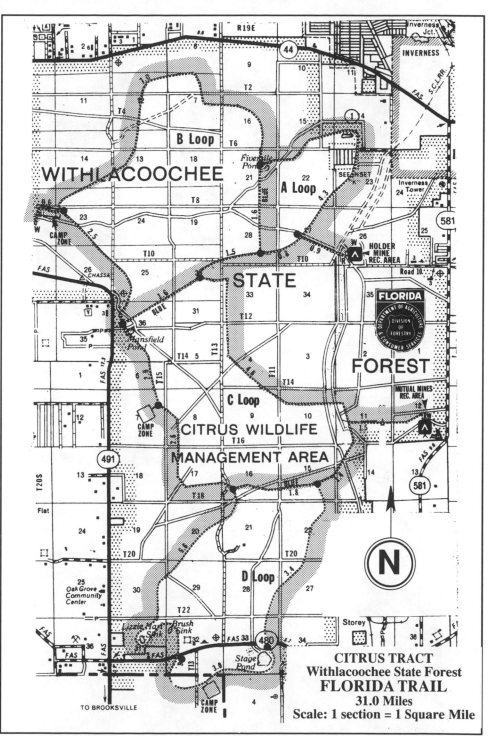

CITRUS TRACT
Withlacoochee State Forest
FLORIDA TRAIL
31.0 Miles
Scale: 1 section = 1 Square Mile

Citrus County

NORTH FLORIDA

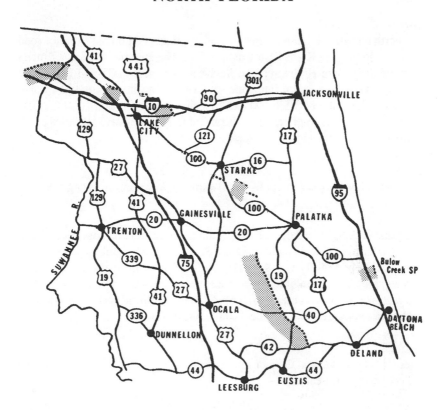

This region includes the Ocala Trail through the beautiful 366,000-acre Ocala National Forest, near Alexander Springs and Juniper Springs. The Gold Head Branch section has a picturesque ravine. Further north the trail follows the Suwannee River.

This part of Florida was home to the Timucuan Indians, whose shell mounds and other artifacts remain in the area. The historic Bellamy Road passed toward the west and pioneer trade moved inland from the coast. The Civil War surged briefly through here, and the southern most battle of the war occurred at Olustee on land close to the Florida Trail. The Suwannee, St. Johns and Oklawaha Rivers were alive with steamboats then, and during the Civil War rebel gunboats prowled the rivers, hid in coves, and fought with cavalry patrols on the river banks.

Bulow Creek State Park

Location
The north terminus is 0.9 mile east of County Road 2001 on the entrance road to Bulow Plantation Ruins State Historic Site. The entrance road is 1.7 miles north of Old Dixie Highway. The intersection of CR 2001 and Old Dixie Highway is 0.9 mile east of Interstate 95, Exit 90. The entrance road may also be reached from the I-95 SR-100 exit by going east to CR 2001 (old CR 5A) and then south. The south terminus is on Old Dixie Highway, 1.1 miles south of the Walter Boardman Lane intersection.

Type of Hiking
The trail is level. Some portions flood during heavy rains or spring tides.

Parking
Trailhead parking is on the south side of the park entrance road outside the gate to Bulow Plantation Ruins State Historic Site. Look for the Bulow Woods Trail sign. Hikers parking before 9 a.m. and after 5 p.m. must use the trailhead parking. Parking is available inside the gates during open hours. The historic site gate is open from nine a.m. to five p.m. South trailhead parking is available at Ormond Fairchild Oak, adjacent to the ranger station.

Water
There is potable water at the picnic area inside the gate. Surface water must be boiled, filtered or treated.

Conveniences
Supplies: Near I-95 Exit 90
Mail: Ormond 32074
Motels: Bunnell, Ormond Beach, I-95, US 1
Public Campgrounds: Tomoka River and Flagler Beach State Parks
Emergency
Flagler County Sheriff: 904-437-4106
Volusia County Sheriff: 904-677-4645
Park Ranger: 904-439-2219

Precautions
Trail blazes are white for the main loop and blue for other trails. Check for ticks after hiking.

Restrictions
Do not pick flowers or plants. The trail is open from sunrise to sunset.

Description
Florida acquired Bulow Creek State Park in 1981 to preserve one of the best remaining stands of live oak along the Florida east coast. The trail starts in a young forest. After a short distance, the trees become larger and the canopy reaches high overhead. This is an old-growth hammock; some of the live oaks are over 200 years old. An old plantation road and several stream crossings add further interest to this section of Bulow Woods. The trail then swings north along the creek and east, finally emerging at Marsh Point for a panoramic view of the pristine marsh. The trail traces higher ground through loblolly pine and magnolia trees. Further south, the trail follows the Cisco Ditch, which has a small waterfall over a limestone outcrop. The blue cross-trail through a pine forest can shorten the loop hike. The park address is P. O. Box 655, Bunnell, FL 32010.

Trail Data - Bulow Creek State Park

Mileage S to N		Mileage N to S
6.2 (1)	Trail terminus at parking area on park road 0.9 mi. east of highway C2001. Look for Bulow Woods Trail sign. Trail follows jeep road.	0.0
6.0	Cross bridge over intermittent stream.	0.2
5.8	Pass white marker denoting plantation cart road. (circa 1825).	0.4
5.5	Cross stream on bridge. Trail route follows meandering stream.	0.7
5.4	Trail turns. Pass through old oak hammock for 0.4 mile.	0.8
5.0	Turn at bridge over intermittent stream.	1.2
4.7	Cross stream and island on two bridges.	1.5
4.4	Junction with blue-blazed cross trail to south Trail follows edge of marsh	1.8
4.2	Panoramic view at Marsh Point. Follow trace of abandoned jeep road.	2.0
3.4	Trail turns. Route follows survey cut through woods and along Cisco Ditch.	2.8
3.1	Pass junction with blue-blazed cross trail to north.	3.1
2.9	Cross Cisco Ditch on log bridge near limestone rapids. Trail parallels Cisco ditch.	3.3
2.7	Junction with Bear Den woods road.	3.5
2.2	Cross power line.	4.0
1.9	Trail crosses paved road (Walter Boardman Lane). Trail follows woods road (Mound Grove Road).	4.3
1.4	Route turns at junction of Mound Grove and Estuary woods roads. Pass junction with blue-blazed 0.5 mile to campsite. Follow east-west Estuary Road across marsh on bridge.	4.8
0.6	Trail turns at Estuary Road junction with woods road near sugar cane patch.	5.6
0.0	South terminus northwest of coquina building on north side of Ormond-Fairchild Oaks parking area.	6.2

BULOW CREEK
State Park
FLORIDA TRAIL
6.2 Miles
Scale: 1 section = 1 Square Mile

Flagler, Volusia Counties

Ocala National Forest-South

Location
The southern terminus is at Clearwater Lake Campground, six miles east of Altoona on CR 42. The northern terminus is at Juniper Springs Recreation Area on SR 40, four miles west of the SR 19 intersection.

Type of Hiking
The Ocala National Forest offers mostly dry, level hiking through pine and hardwood forest, along the edges of prairies and near a jungle swamp. It is a beautiful part of the Florida National Scenic Trail.

Parking
Park at the campgrounds at either terminus. At the south terminus and at Alexander Springs, turn right into the trail parking lot before the entrance booth. There is a parking fee at Juniper Springs.

Water
Potable water is available at each terminus, at Alexander Springs, at the Paisley Fire Tower and at Farles Prairie campsite. Surface water should be boiled, filtered or treated.

Conveniences
Supplies: Altoona, Paisley and at Juniper Springs concession
Mail: Ocala 32670 or Astor 32002
Motels: Astor, Ocala
Public Campgrounds: Juniper Springs, Alexander Springs, Clearwater Lake

Emergency
Lake County Sheriff: 904-343-950
Marion County Sheriff: 904-732-8181
US Forest Service Seminole Ranger District: 904-357-3721

Precautions
Limit backpacking groups to no more than 12 people.

Restrictions
Do not build fires during drought conditions.

Description

The south part of the Ocala National Forest is composed mostly of long leaf yellow pine "islands" scattered among sand pine and other short leaf pines. There are also areas with oaks, maples and other hardwoods, along with blueberry, gallberry and other shrubs. This trail skirts many prairies: shallow, grassy ponds hundreds of yards in diameter. Grassy prairies are good places to observe wildlife.

A side trip on the blue-blazed trail to beautiful, crystal clear Alexander Springs (78 million gallons per day) is highly recommended for those who would like to stop for a snack, or a swim in the cool spring water. Portions of the forest near Alexander Springs, Billies Bay and Juniper Prairie are designated wilderness areas.

The Florida Trail began in the Ocala National Florida in 1966. The trail through the forest is the crown jewel of the Florida Trail system.

Trail Data - Ocala South

Mileage S to N		Mileage N to S
27.6 (3)	North terminus at Juniper Springs Recreation Area. Water, swimming, concession, camping.	0.0
26.3	Cross SR 40.	1.3
26.0	Trail crosses marsh on boardwalk.	1.6
22.3	Cross FR 599.	5.3
22.0	Panoramic view of Farles Prairie north rim. Campsite.	5.0
19.6	Cross FR 595. Farles Prairie campsite 0.1 mile east on blue-blazed trail. Water, latrines.	8.0
17.6	Junction with north end of blue-blazed loop trail around east side of Buck Lake. Water, camping 0.1 mile east. FT continues on west side of lake.	10.0
17.2	Short side trail to west edge of Buck Lake.	10.4
16.7	Junction with south end of blue-blazed loop trail around east side of Buck Lake.	10.9
15.8	Trail crosses graded County Road 9277 (Railroad Grade Road).	11.8
14.9	Trail crosses SR 19 (paved).	12.7
12.9	Cross FR 525. Trail skirts south side of Billies Bay Wilderness.	14.7
11.3	Cross SR 445 (paved).	16.3
11.1 (2)	Blue-blazed side trail to Alexander Springs (0.5 mile) joins from northeast. Water, camping (fee).	16.5
9.5	Cross long boardwalk.	18.1
6.9	Cross FR 539.	20.7
6.7	Trail crosses swamp on several short boardwalks.	20.9
5.4	Cross power line right-of-way.	22.2
4.9	Cross creek on boardwalk.	22.7
2.2	Cross FR 538.	25.4
1.5	Trail crosses woods road. Paisley Fire Tower visible.	26.1
0.5	GOLDEN BLAZE TREE. 1986 commemoration of twenty years of building the Florida Trail.	27.1
0.3 (1)	Blue-blazed side trail to Clearwater Lake Campground trailhead. Water, swimming, camping (fee).	27.3
0.0	Southern terminus at CR 42 south of Paisley just east of entrance to Clearwater Lake Recreation Area. Ocala Trail sign on north side of CR 42.	27.6

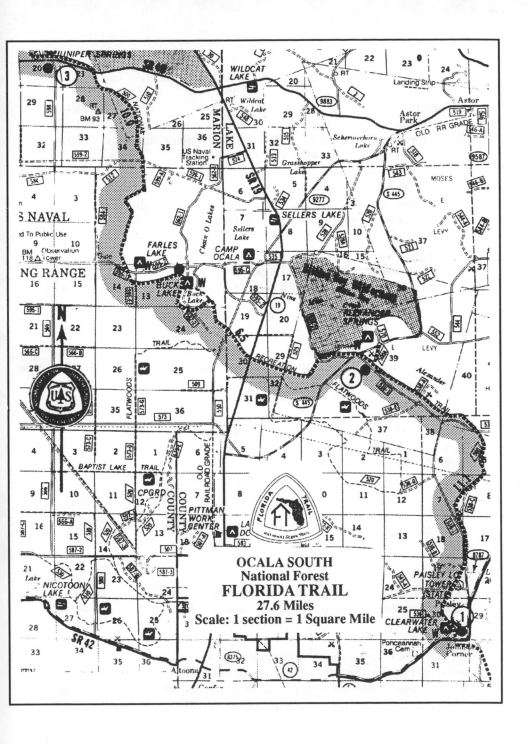

OCALA SOUTH
National Forest
FLORIDA TRAIL
27.6 Miles
Scale: 1 section = 1 Square Mile

Marion County

OCALA NATIONAL FOREST - NORTH

Location

The southern terminus is at Juniper Springs Recreation Area on SR 40, four miles west of the SR 19 intersection. The northern terminus is at the Barge Canal at St. John's Lock, off SR 19.

Type of Hiking

This section offers mostly level, dry hiking through pine islands and hardwood forest and along the edges of "prairies" and ponds.

Parking

At the northern terminus, park at the lock (rest rooms are available). At the southern terminus, park at Juniper Springs Recreation Area. A fee will be charged.

Water

Potable water is available at Juniper Springs, Hopkins Prairie, Rodman Dam and Salt Springs. Surface water and well water at Lake Delancey should be boiled, filtered or treated.

Conveniences

Supplies: Astor, Salt Springs, Silver Springs, Ft. McCoy
Mail: Silver Springs 32688, Ft. McCoy 32637
Motels: Astor, Salt Springs, Silver Springs
Public Campgrounds: Juniper Springs, Rodman Dam, Salt Springs

Emergency

Marion County Sheriff: 904-732-9111
US Forest Service: 904-625-2520

Restrictions

Do not build fires during drought conditions. Camping in hunting areas during general hunting season is permitted only at designated sites.

Description

The north part of the Ocala forest is mostly pine mixed with a variety of hardwoods and shrubs. The trail skirts ponds and several large prairies. Trail work in the Juniper Prairie Wilderness must be done with hand tools only. FTA workers use two-man crosscut saws to remove blown down trees on this section of the trail. A blue-blazed side trail to Salt Springs leads to a store, restaurant and a spring for swimming. Juniper Springs is also good for swimming, and the Juniper Spring run is a great short canoe trip. Canoes and shuttle service are available at the park concession.

The north end of this portion of the Florida Trail gives hikers an opportunity to see the now abandoned attempt made by man to change the Oklawaha River basin to the Cross Florida Barge Canal.

Trail Data - Ocala North

Mileage S to N		Mileage N to S
	Access road to lock intersects SR19 about 8 miles south of Palatka.	
46.2 ④	Trail crosses Barge Canal lock. Parking, water. Lock can be crossed between 8 a.m. and 5 p.m. all week. South gate normally locked. Use whistle to attract attendant's attention. Follow Barge Canal embankment under bridge.	0.0
41.3	Trail turns through steel gate at dip in embankment. Follow dirt service road.	4.9
41.1	Trail turns at junction with service road.	5.1
40.7	Pass through campground entrance. Water.	5.5
39.5 ③	Spillway at Rodman Dam. Rodman Recreation Area 1.2 miles north. Camping (fee), water.	6.7
38.5	Trail follows unmarked forest road near Penner Ponds for 1.0 mile.	7.7
37.1	Cross FR 77.	9.1
35.7	Cross FR 31. North border of Riverside Island.	10.5
34.1	Cross FR 88.	12.1
32.0	Cross FR 75 at Lake Delancey. Water (must be treated), camping, latrines.	14.2
28.4	Cross south border Riverside Island.	17.8
27.7	Pass Grassy Pond. Water, Camping, Latrines.	18.5
26.8	Cross FR 88.	19.4
26.1	Cross CR 316. North Hunt headquarters. Water.	20.1

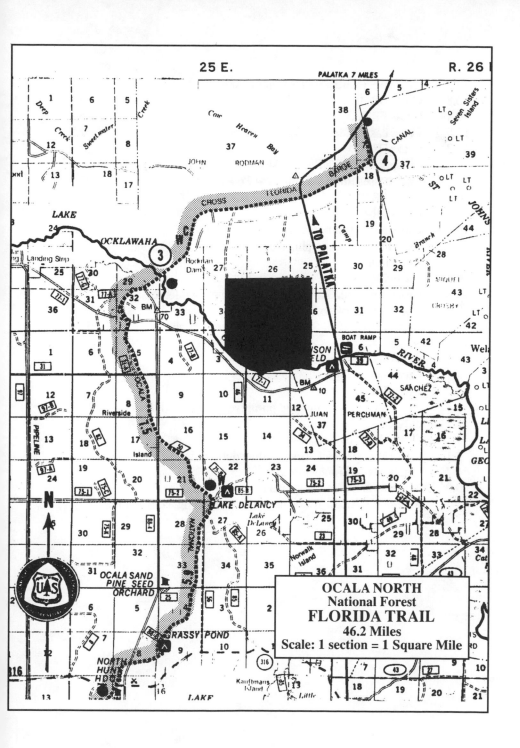

Putnam, Marion Counties

22.2	Cross west border Salt Springs Island.	24.0
20.8	Cross CR 314.	25.4
20.4	Cross FR 88.	25.8
18.9	Cross east border Salt Springs Island.	27.3
17.7	Cross FR 51.	28.5
16.9 ②	Junction with Salt Springs side trail. 3.0 miles.	29.3
16.7	Trail passes through Long Leaf Ponds.	29.5
16.0	Cross FR 90.	30.2
15.7	Cross FR 65.	30.5
15.5	Cross northwest border Hopkins' Prairie.	30.7
11.0	Hopkins Prairie camping area. Water, camping, latrine, swimming.	35.2
9.9	Cross FR 86.	36.3
8.8	Cross north side Pat's Island. Trail enters wilderness area. North border of no hunting area.	37.4
8.2	Cross FR 10. (Old Silver Glen Springs to Grahamville Road).	38.0
8.1	Cross south side Pat's Island.	38.1
7.1	Cross north edge of Juniper Prairie.	39.1
5.7	Cross FR 76.	40.5
5.4	Hidden Pond. Swimming, primitive campsites (hikers only).	40.8
4.2	Cross Whiskey Creek.	42.0
3.1	Cross Whispering Creek. Wading during high water.	43.1
1.7	South edge of Juniper Prairie.	44.5
0.0 ①	South terminus at entry road to Juniper Springs Recreation Area. Water, camping, swimming, concession.	46.2

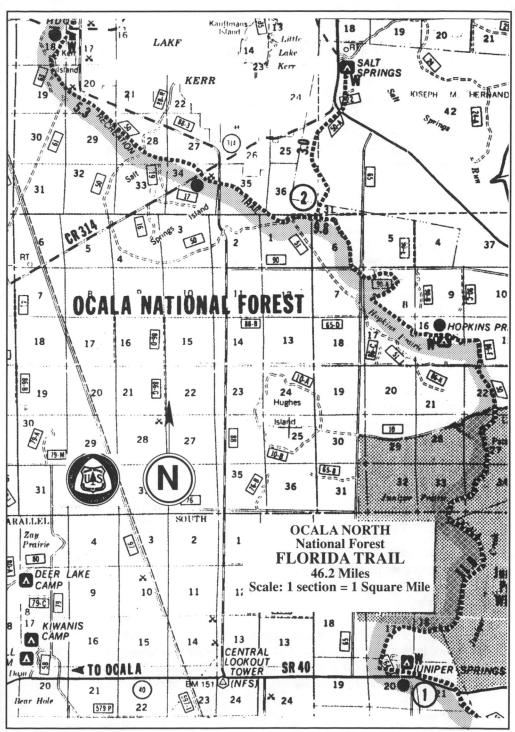

OCALA NORTH
National Forest
FLORIDA TRAIL
46.2 Miles
Scale: 1 section = 1 Square Mile

Putnam, Marion Counties

Gold Head Branch

Location
The trail is located within Gold Head Branch State Park.

Type of Hiking
The trail includes streams, sandhills, ridges and a deep ravine.   Gold Head Branch State Park's scenic ravine trail adjoins the Florida Trail.

Parking
Park at Gold Head Branch State Park.

Water
Potable water is available in the park.

Conveniences
Supplies: Georges Lake, Hampton, Keystone Heights
Mail: Keystone Heights 32656
Motels: Keystone Heights
Public Campgrounds: Gold Head Branch State Park

Emergency
Putnam County Sheriff: 904-328-3405
Clay County Sheriff: 904-284-7575
Bradford County Sheriff: 904-964-6280

Precautions
The primitive campsite in the park must be reserved (limit, 12 overnight backpackers). Call 904-473-4701 or write Gold Head Branch State Park, Rt. 1, Box 545, Keystone Heights, FL 32656.

Restrictions
Campfires are permitted only in fire rings.

Description
This section passes through hilly "sandhill" terrain with forests of longleaf pine and turkey oak, through densely forested areas with different kinds of hardwood trees and shrubs, and through pine plantations in various growth stages. Wildlife includes pocket gophers, grey foxes and squirrels. The park provides swimming in Lake Johnson, and a deep ravine shaded by sweet gum, magnolia

and oaks, and carpeted with ferns. In the pine woods along the trail look for "catfaces" (the scars on pine trees left by the turpentine industry) and for red clay turpentine pots which look like flower pots. The trail is part of the Florida Recreational Trails System.

Trail Data - Gold Head Branch

Mileage N to S			Mileage S to N
3.2	①	Pass entrance to Gold Head Branch State Park. Water. Register here for camping. White-blazed trail is north of main park roads.	0.0
2.4		Pass Deer Lake. Trail passes through Gold Head Branch ravine.	0.8
1.0	②	Cross Gold Head Branch on Bridge. Side trail to primitive campsite.	2.2
0.8		Trail passes picnic, swimming area. Water.	2.4
0.0	③	Public trail ends at pass through stile at south boundary of Gold Head Branch State Park.	3.2

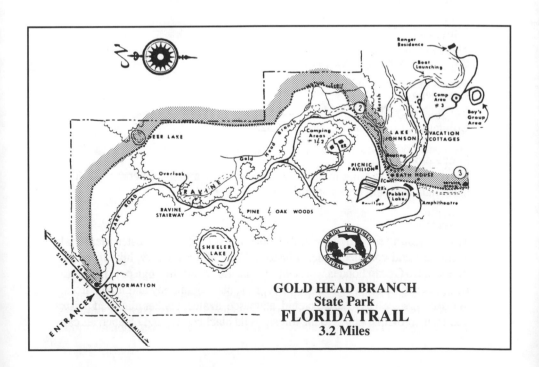

GOLD HEAD BRANCH
State Park
FLORIDA TRAIL
3.2 Miles

Clay County

Osceola National Forest

Location
The east terminus is 15 miles east of Lake City on US 90 at the Olustee fire tower. The West terminus is at the intersection of US 441 and Drew Grade Road.

Type of Hiking
This is a flat trail leading through pine and hardwood forest and across many streams. Some wading may be necessary in the rainy season.

Parking
Park at the Olustee Fire Tower at the east end.

Water
There is potable water at the Olustee Battlefield Museum and at Ocean Pond Campground. Ground water and water from the west tower must be boiled, filtered or treated.

Conveniences
Supplies: Olustee, Lake City
Mail: Lake City 32055
Motels: Lake City
Public Campgrounds: Ocean Pond

Emergengcy
Baker County Sheriff: 904-259-2231
Columbia County Sheriff: 904-752-3223

Precautions
Blazes may be missing in clear-cut areas. Carry a map and compass. The battlefield museum opens at nine a.m.

Description
This interesting section of the trail offers forest hiking. The Olustee Memorial at the east end commemorates a historic Civil War battle. A hike from the memorial to Ocean Pond is worthwhile. The trail winds through pine palmetto flatlands and through swamps with cypress, black gum, bay and maple trees. Wildflowers such as rosebud orchid, atamasco, azalea, pitcher plant and phlox add their colorful touches to the forest. Wild blackberries and blueberries can

be picked some places in late spring. In the Osceola Forest old "borrow pits" (soil excavation sites) have filled with water, creating many small ponds. These make attractive spots for lunch, rest or camping. One very scenic pond is on the trail near Ocean Pond. Thanks to the U.S. Forest Service, there are now 30 small bridges and catwalks over tributary streams which hikers once had to wade.

HIKERS BEWARE!!

If you are hiking through the Olustee and Osceola National Forest sections during the middle of each February, be on the lookout for enemy scouts, infantry and artillery! You may detect the characteristic odor of gunpowder if the wind is right. The reason will be the annual re-enactment of the Civil War Battle of Olustee fought near Ocean Pond on February 20, 1864. The actual re-enactment takes place near the Musuem on US 90 east of the town of Olustee. The people of Lake City and Columbia County host this festival every year and the realism is excellent.

There is also street dancing, a parade, a Fun Run, and lots of good food. Everyone is invited but don't wear a Civil War cap unless you are ready to do combat with the other side!

Trail Data - Osceola

Mileage E to W		Mileage W to E
21.5	US 441 - Drew Grade Road Junction. Follow Drew Grade Road for 1.1 Miles.	0.0
20.4 ④	Trail at Osceola NF boundary at pass-through at road. Follow jeep road through woods for 1.2 miles.	1.1
19.2	Cross FR 237.	2.3
16.4 ③	Cross FR 233 0.2 miles east of West Tower. Water, campsite, latrine.	5.1
14.7	Trail follows FR 234.	6.8
14.1	Trail follows old jeep road. Campsite.	7.4
10.5	Cross paved road CR 250.	11.0
8.2	Cross CR 250A. Pass-throughs on both sides.	13.3
6.9	Cross FR 263B.	14.6
6.6	Trail crosses I-10 on SR 250A Bridge.	14.9
5.6 ②	Junction with 0.5 mile blue-blazed trail to Ocean Pond Campground (fee). Water, latrines, swimming.	15.9
5.1	Cross SR 250A.	16.4
4.2	Cross forest road. Campsight.	17.3
3.4	Cross forest road.	18.1
1.3	Trail leaves/enters woods. Follow CR 208 for 0.7 mile.	20.2
0.6	Trail leaves/enters woods.	20.9
0.3	Campsight on south side of east-west road. Trail follows east-west road past Olustee Tower.	21.2
0.0 ①	East terminus. US 90 entrance to Olustee Memorial. Water, restroom.	21.5

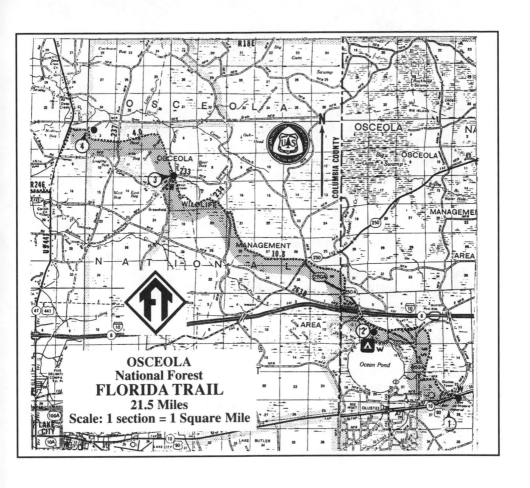

OSCEOLA
National Forest
FLORIDA TRAIL
21.5 Miles
Scale: 1 section = 1 Square Mile

Baker, Columbia Counties

Stephen Foster

Location
The trail is within the Stephen Foster State Folklore Center in White Springs.

Type of Hiking
This trail affords almost continuous views of the Suwannee River, passing along the river, over hills, through deep forests and small ravines. In the spring flood stage wading may be necessary.

Parking
Park at the eastern terminus at the Stephen Foster Folklore Center.

Water
There is potable water at the Folklore Center. River water should be boiled, filtered or treated.

Conveniences
Supplies: White Springs
Mail: White Springs 32096
Motels: White Springs
Public Campgrounds: Suwannee River State Park

Emergency
Hamilton County Sheriff: 904-792-1001

Description
This section of the trail runs almost continuously beside the Suwannee River. The trail has been designated part of the Florida Recreational Trails System. The Suwannee's tea-colored water, stained by the cypress trees, is fed by springs. You will see clear patches where these springs enter the river. The striking white sand beaches along the Suwannee make perfect places to camp or swim.

Along the trail you will see impressive clusters of huge cypresses and oak trees amid swamps. White lillies, azalea, sparkleberries, dogwood and redbud trees grow along the path. Otter, beaver, deer and many water birds may be seen. Be sure to notice the high water marks posted along the river. These record impressive floods of years past. The town of White Springs is an interesting place to visit, with a restaurant and a local crafts outlet. The Stephen Foster Center offers historic exhibits and a carillon tower. The Florida Folk Festival is held there each year over the Memorial Day weekend.

Trail Data - Stephen Foster

Mileage E to W		Mileage W to E
4.1	Public trail (white blazes) stops/starts at park boundary.	0.0
3.6	Junction of trail with river. Trail enters/leaves woods.	0.5
0.9	Cross cable right of way.	3.2
0.7	Cross boundary of Stephen Foster Folklore Center.	3.4
0.0	East terminus at gate of Stephen Foster Folklore Center.	4.1

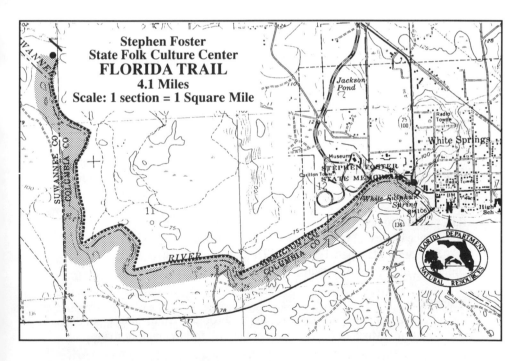

Stephen Foster
State Folk Culture Center
FLORIDA TRAIL
4.1 Miles
Scale: 1 section = 1 Square Mile

Hamilton County

ELLAVILLE / SUWANNEE RIVER

Location
The Ellaville section is located along the Withlacoochee and Suwannee rivers and on graded public roads in Madison County. The west terminus of the Ellaville trail is on SR 53, seven miles south of the I-10 interchange. The east terminus is at the Withlacoochee River bridge on CR 141 near Suwannee River State Park. The trail continues east for 4.6 miles within park land on the north side of the river. The trail within the park is part of the Florida Recreational Trails System.

Parking
Park at Suwannee River State Park, or at the Florida Agricultural Inspection Station near the Suwannee River bridge. Take the first dirt road to the right north of the river on CR 141 for closer access to the east terminus in SRSP. Park near boat ramp at mile 2.2.

Water
Potable water is available from the Agricultural Inspection Station and at Suwannee River State Park. Boil, filter or treat river water.

Conveniences
Supplies: Near Suwannee River State Park and at I-10 and route 90 interchanges.
Mail: Lee 32059
Motels: Perry
Public Campgrounds: Suwannee River State Park

Emergency
Madison County Sheriff: 904-973-4151.

Precautions
Blazes on the graded roads part of this section are limited to intersections with "confidence blazes" at irregular intervals. The trail is blazed white east of CR 141. Stop at the state park boundary. The blazes change to orange on private land. FTA membership is required to hike in private areas.

Description
The Ellaville trail follows the Suwannee through terrain similar to the preceding trail. Much of the west part of the trail follows county roads.

Trail Data - Ellaville

Mileage E to W			Mileage W to E
16.7	①	East terminus at Withlacoochee River Bridge at CR 141.	0.0
16.6		Trail register.	0.1
15.7		Old campsite on Withlacoochee River.	1.0
15.0		Go around big oak tree. Note cable left from logging days.	1.7
14.9		Cross railroad track and old Rt. 90. Campground and water, 1,000 feet east.	1.8
14.7		Cross US 90.	2.0
14.4		Bluff campsite on Suwannee River.	2.3
12.6		Go under four power lines.	4.1
12.1		Trail leaves river, parallels I-10.	4.6
10.6	②	Cross I-10 on overpass (River Ranch Road).	6.1
9.2		Trail passes abandoned homestead.	7.5
7.1		Trail turns back onto state land.	9.6
6.8		Trail follows fire lane.	9.9
5.8		Old boat ramp and picnic table.	10.9
5.4	③	Campsite on river.	11.3
5.1		Trail turns and follows fence.	11.6
4.3		Cross River Ranch Road. Follow graded road next four miles.	12.4
1.9		Cross CR 255. Continue on graded road.	14.8
0.5		Turn on old log road.	16.2
0.0	④	West terminus at SR 53.	16.7

Trail Data - Suwannee River State Park

Mileage W to E			Mileage E to W
4.6	①	West terminus at Withlacoochee River bridge on CR 141. Trail follows cleared area.	0.0
4.1		Suwannee River State Park boundary. White blazes in park.	0.5
3.4		Cross under power lines.	1.2
2.9		Trail junction with Suwannee River.	1.7
2.2	②	Trail passes by boat ramp. Public road access.	2.4
2.1		Underground stream surfaces in two deep sinkholes. Trail by the river.	2.5
0.0		Suwannee River State Park boundary. White blazes in park.	4.6

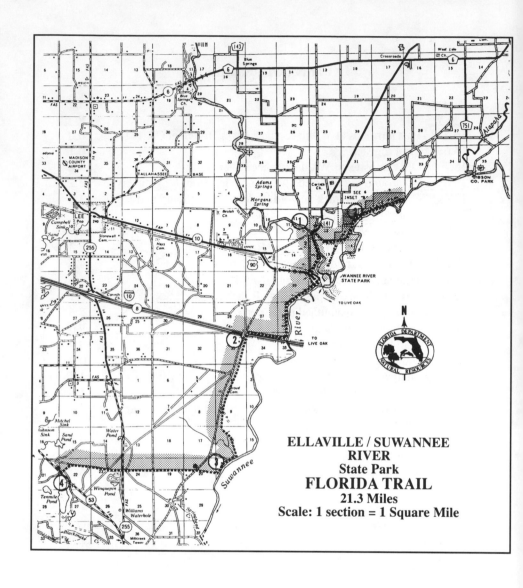

ELLAVILLE / SUWANNEE
RIVER
State Park
FLORIDA TRAIL
21.3 Miles
Scale: 1 section = 1 Square Mile

Hamilton, Madison Counties

PANHANDLE

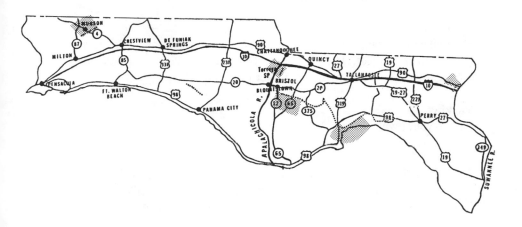

This area extends from the Suwannee River across Florida's panhandle. It connects the Gulf states to peninsular Florida, and has been heavily traveled since the days of the aboriginal Indians. These Indians, Spanish explorers, northern settlers, and Civil War soldiers passed through here. This part of the state offers a varied terrain: Gulf shore salt marshes, spring-fed cypress swamps, sandy pine woods, high-rolling hills and spectacular ravines and bluffs. The titi wilderness in the Apalachicola Forest and the thickets in Bradwell Bay will test skills with map and compass. The hills of Torreya are a warm up for the Appalachian Trail. The trail through St. Marks National Wildlife Refuge offers sweeping vistas of great salt marshes stretching to the horizon. Part of the trail (in Blackwater River State Forest) follows General Andrew Jackson's military route.

Aucilla River

Location
The east terminus is at a forest road 1.75 miles west of CR 14. The road connects with CR 14 one mile south of the Aucilla River bridge. The west terminus is 0.75 miles west of the US 98 bridge over the Aucilla River. The west end of the sinks is 5.8 miles northeast of the US 98 bridge.

Type of Hiking
The trail leads through limestone sinks in the south portion and along the river berm in the north part. Hiking is dry except when the river is at flood stage (check at the Cabbage Grove Fire Tower for conditions).

Parking
Park at your own risk.

Water
There is potable water at Cabbage Grove Fire Tower, 2.6 miles south of the SR 14 trail crossing. Water is also available at the Dolomite mines trailer on Powell Hammock Road and at Nutall Rise. Boil, filter or treat river and surface water.

Conveniences
Supplies: Lamont
Mail: Lamont 32336
Motels: Perry
Public Campgrounds: Goose Pasture (Wacissa River), primitive, no potable water. Closed during general hunting season.

Emergency
Taylor County Sheriff: 904-584-4225
Florida Division of Forestry: 904-584-6121 (Perry)
Game and Fish Commission: 904-488-6254

Precautions
Plan carefully for this remote section of trail. Carry a map and compass. Flood waters can make this trail hazardous because it runs close to the edges of sinks and along the river berm. High water can obscure boundaries. Use care crossing sloughs. Check the general hunting season dates and wear safety orange during general hunting season.

Restrictions

Backcountry camping is not permitted during general hunting season. The trail is closed to hikers during the first nine days of general hunting season, the Thanksgiving weekend, and the week between Christmas and New Year holidays.

Description

This is a unique section because of the curious fate of the Aucilla River. Emerging from swamps near the state border, the river flows southwestward, passing over the Aucilla Rapids and then disappears underground one half mile north of Goose Pasture Road. For a distance of eight miles, the river appears and disappears in a series of "rises" and "sinks." The river continues this pattern until the final rise at Nutall Rise 0.5 mile north of the US 98 bridge. Day hikes along the sinks can start at the trail crossing on Goose Pasture Road. Look for FT signs near the cattle grate. The sinks are numbered in the following trail data and correspond to numbers on blazes on each side of the sinks.

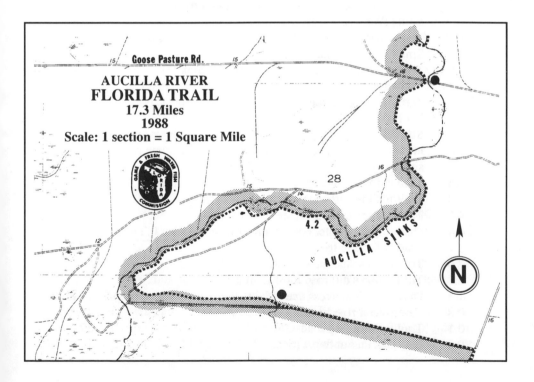

Goose Pasture Rd.

AUCILLA RIVER
FLORIDA TRAIL
17.3 Miles
1988
Scale: 1 section = 1 Square Mile

28

4.2

AUCILLA SINKS

N

Trail Data - Aucilla River

Mileage E to W		Description	Mileage W to E
17.3	①	West terminus on Aucilla River US 98 bridge (Jefferson county line). Follow highway 0.75 miles west for St. Marks trailhead. Follow US 98 for two miles.	0.0
15.3	②	Trail turns at intersection of US98 and Powell Hammock Grade Road. Note Dolomite and WMA signs at corner.	2.0
13.2		Trail on road passes dolomite pits. Trail on graded road.	4.1
11.5		Trail at forest edge.	5.8
10.8		Follows jeep and dirt roads.	6.5
10.7		Trail at south junction with sinks. Pass Twin Sinks (16), Sarasinks (15).	6.6
10.2		Trail crosses dirt road. Pass Chocolate Sinks (14), New Sink (13), Mosquito Slap Sink (12), Hurry Up Sink (11).	7.1
9.5		Trail crosses dirt road. Pass Kitchen Sink (10), Long Suffering Sink (9), Ryan Sink (7), Dragonfly Sink (6), Watts Sink (5).	9.5
8.5		Trail crosses dirt road. Pass Frink Sink (4), Sunshine Sink (3), Long Sink (2).	8.8
7.9		Trail crosses dirt road. Pass Breakdown Sink (1).	9.4
7.3		Trail crosses Goose Pasture Road. FT signs. Cross cattle grate. Pass Roadside Sink (1N), Overflow Sink (2N), Vortex Sink (3N).	10.0
7.1		SILVER BLAZE TREE. 1984 commemoration of major north FT connection. Trail on dirt road passes main river sink (4N).	10.2
6.8		Trail at forest edge on river. Some trail on dirt road.	10.5
5.3		Trail/road junction at unimproved boat ramp.	12.0
4.5		Trail at edge of clearcut area.	12.8
4.4		Pass old bridge site. Follow dirt road beside river 0.3 mile.	13.3
3.7		Trail at forest edge.	13.6
2.6		Trail passes Aucilla River Rapids (5N).	14.7
1.7		Trail follows dirt road for 0.15 mile.	15.6
1.5		Pass big bald cypress tree (15.3 ft. circ.) at riverbend (6N).	15.8
0.8		Campsite at riverbend.	16.5
0.1		Trail follows jeep road.	17.2
0.0	③	East terminus at forest road. FT sign. CR 14 1.75 mile E.	17.3

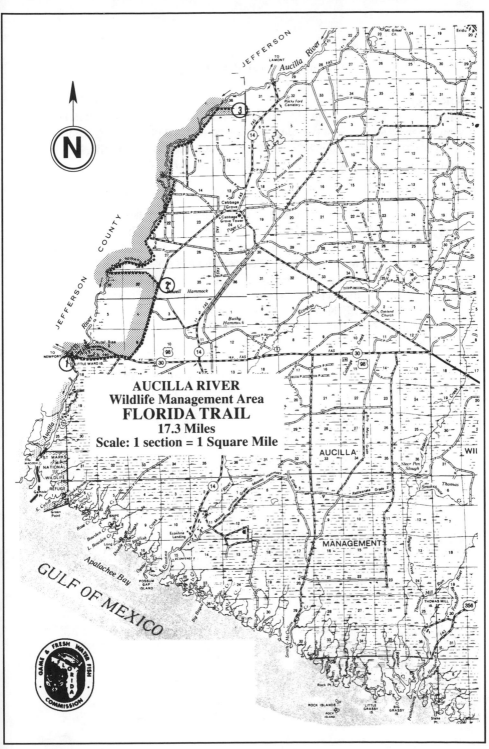

AUCILLA RIVER
Wildlife Management Area
FLORIDA TRAIL
17.3 Miles
Scale: 1 section = 1 Square Mile

Taylor County

St. Marks National Wildlife Refuge

Location
The trail is mostly within the St. Marks National Wildlife Refuge, 20 miles southeast of Tallahassee. The west terminus is on US 319, 1.1 miles west of Medart. The east terminus is on US 98, 0.75 mile west of the Aucilla River bridge, marked only by a double blaze on the road surface.

Type of Hiking
Hiking is dry over most of the trail except during periods of heavy rains. For approximately 15 miles, the trail follows refuge roads which are closed to vehicles and offer easy hiking. Several blue-blazed spur and loop trails extend off the main trail. The trail south of the east terminus is across private land and is not blazed; stay to west on old road bed. To cross the St. Marks River at the town of St. Marks, hikers must get boat passage (ask locally). From the town of St. Marks to US 98, the trail follows the old Tallahassee-St. Marks railroad corridor on the St. Marks Historic State Trail.

Parking
Park at your own risk. Leave nothing visible in your car. There are three designated parking areas: at the west trailhead, at Wakulla Beach Road, and at the Refuge Visitor Center.

Water
There is potable water at the Refuge Visitor Center (follow blue blazes from trail), the canoe rental on the east side of Wakulla River bridge, and in the towns of St. Marks and Spring Creek. Boil, filter or treat all surface water.

Conveniences
Supplies: St. Marks, Spring Creek, Medart, Newport
Mail: St. Marks 32355; Sopchoppy 32358
Motels: Wakulla Springs State Park (Lodge), St. Marks, Spring Creek
Public Campgounds: Ochlockonee State Park, Division of Forestry
                    at Newport

Emergency
Wakulla County Sheriff: 904-926-7171
Game and Fish Commission: 904-488-6254
Refuge Headquarters: 904-925-6121

Precautions

The Newport campground is crowded during hunting season. Insects can be serious. Use repellents for ticks and chiggers. Wear safety orange during general hunting season and Refuge special hunts. The visitor center is open from 8 a.m. to 4:30 p.m. weekdays, and from 10 a.m to 4 p.m. on Sundays. To cross the St. Marks River safely, hail boats from the south bank of the trail or contact Allan Hobbs at Shell Island Fish Camp, 904-925-6226.

Restrictions

Check with the refuge office. The refuge is open during daylight hours only, but campsites are available by reservation for anyone hiking the entire 43 miles. All campers must secure permits from the Refuge Office: P.O. Box 68, St. Marks, FL 32355. No vehicles are permitted on refuge roads, except on hunting weekends. Campfires are not permitted in the refuge or the adjacent area. Plant and live animal collecting, and gathering or digging of historical artifacts are not permitted in the refuge. Freshwater fishing and crabbing are permitted in the refuge during daylight hours. Parts of the trail may be closed to hikers during refuge hunting weekends. Write or call the refuge for dates and restrictions.

Description

The trail through the St. Marks NWR traverses a greater variety of forest types and wildlife zones than any other north Florida section of the trail. Besides its rich forests of longleaf pine and turkey oak, the refuge shelters old growth mesic and hydric hardwood forests, cypress and gum swamps, beech-magnolia groves, cabbage palm/live oak hammocks, and the seemingly endless expanses of salt marshes along the coastal fringe. For about seven miles on the east side of the refuge, the trail follows a series of dikes built to impound freshwater for the thousands of waterfowl which winter here. Southern bald eagles, ospreys, otters, alligators, turkeys, fox squirrels, raccoons and whitetailed deer can be seen. More than 300 species of birds have been counted at the refuge and 98 of these have nested there.

In addition to its rich natural history, this area abounds in the human record. Indian mounds dating back more than 2,000 years are scattered along the coastline and up the Aucilla River. Fort San Marcos de Apalachee in St. Marks town was established by the Spanish in 1679 and has been occupied by pirates, British, Confederate and Federal forces since. The area has a State Museum 0.2 miles west of the Rail-Trail in the town of St. Marks. It is well worth a side hike. Remnants of Confederate salt evaporation kettles can be found at several points in the salt marshes. There are small isolated mounds in the salt marshes covered with red cedar and cabbage palms; on the mounds you may find evidence of bricks used to construct the kilns and perhaps fragments of iron from the kettles used to evaporate the water. Several segments of the trail follow abandoned railroad beds, or "tram roads," built shortly after the turn of the century for the purpose of logging the virgin cypress and pine forests still found along the Florida Gulf coast. The trail, upon entering the refuge on the east, follows a spur and then the main line of the Aucilla Tram Road; in most places, however, these old railroad beds have been converted into refuge roads and are no longer distinguishable.

The trail in the St. Marks Refuge also passes through two federally designated wilderness areas: along the west side of the Aucilla River and continuing along the south side of the trail along the dikes; and along the east side of the St. Marks River where the trail follows the old road bed north from Port Leon. Old Port Leon was the site of a town and deepwater port that was built in 1842 and abandoned in 1848 after a devastating hurricane. In 1936 old port Leon became the site for the first headquarters of the newly created St. Marks Refuge. The fire tower still stands south of this spot.

Port Leon was once connected to Tallahassee by the first chartered and second built railroad in Florida's history. The railroad segment between Port Leon and the town of St. Marks was also abandoned after the 1848 hurricane. The remaining 20 mile segment stayed in use until it was abandoned in 1984. Florida then purchased 16 miles of the old railroad to construct the state's first hiker-biker recreation trail. The trail follows this route for 1.6 miles to US 98. At the Wakulla River and US 98, there is a canoe rental. Several days spent paddling these rivers and exploring the salt marshes is well worth the layover time. The best trail access points for day hikes are the trailhead off US 319, Wakulla Beach Road or Lighthouse Road (SR 59). The Florida Trail through the St. Marks Refuge was among the first sections designated in 1988 as Florida National Scenic Trail.

Trail Data - St. Marks

Mileage E to W		Mileage W to E
43.4 ①	West terminus on US 319. Look for FNST sign. Follow highway 0.3 mile west to Apalachicola NF trail.	0.0
42.2	Cross US 98. Grocery, laundry to north.	1.2
40.6	Trail joins-leaves graded sand road (Purifying Creek Road).	2.8
40.3	Trail crosses graded road.	3.1
38.9	Trail reaches marsh point. Blue-glazed trail to view of salt marshes. Marsh point campsite.	4.5
37.5	Cross grass road. Pass blue-blazed two mile side trail to FT and Purifying Creek Road.	5.9
37.1	Cross Spring Creek on foot bridge.	6.3
36.7	Follow sand road for 0.6 mile.	6.7
35.2	Trail junction with CR 365. Refuge boundary. Seafood restaurant, motel and grocery 1.3 miles south at village of Spring Creek. Follow paved road for 1.7 miles.	8.2
33.5	Cross Refuge boundary gate. Trail follows sand road for 0.9 mile.	9.9
31.1	Pass blue-blazed path to Blue Springs,	12.3
31.6	Wakulla Field campsite is in the SE corner of old field	12.8
30.1	Trail-grass road junction. Pass blue three-mile loop to FT and CR 365. Follow boundary road for 1.7 mile.	13.3
28.4	Cross graded sand road (Wakulla Beach Road) at gate. Trail follows road to avoid swamp. River Hammock Campsite.	15.0
25.5	Pass sawdust pile. Cross Refuge boundary fence. Pass blue-blazed loop (2 miles) to FT and Wakulla Beach Road. Follow jeep road 1.2 miles through private land.	18.1
24.2	Trail junction. US 98 and jeep road. Double blaze on pole. Cross posted cable gate.	19.2
23.9	Cross Wakulla River on US 98. Water at canoe rental. Follow US 98 for 2.3 miles.	19.5
21.6 ②	Junction with US 98 and Tallahassee-St. Marks Hiker-Biker trail. Trail follows Hiker-Biker trail for 1.7 miles to town of St. Marks. Food, lodging, supplies available.	21.8

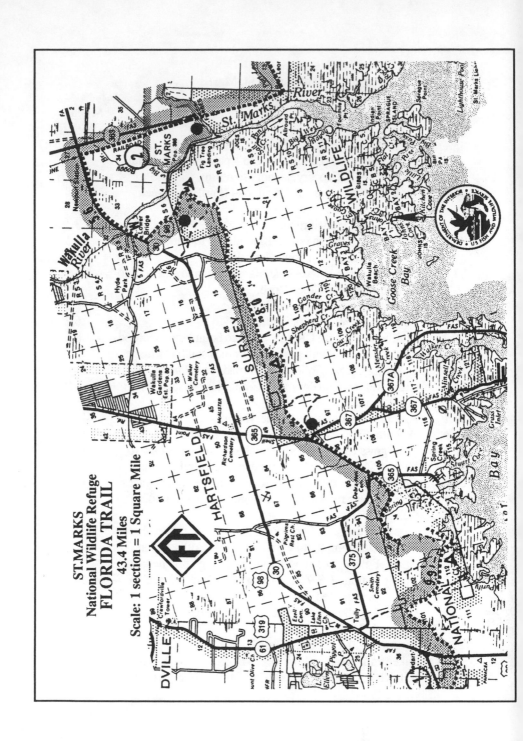

ST. MARKS
National Wildlife Refuge
FLORIDA TRAIL
43.4 Miles
Scale: 1 section = 1 Square Mile

Jefferson, Wakulla Counties

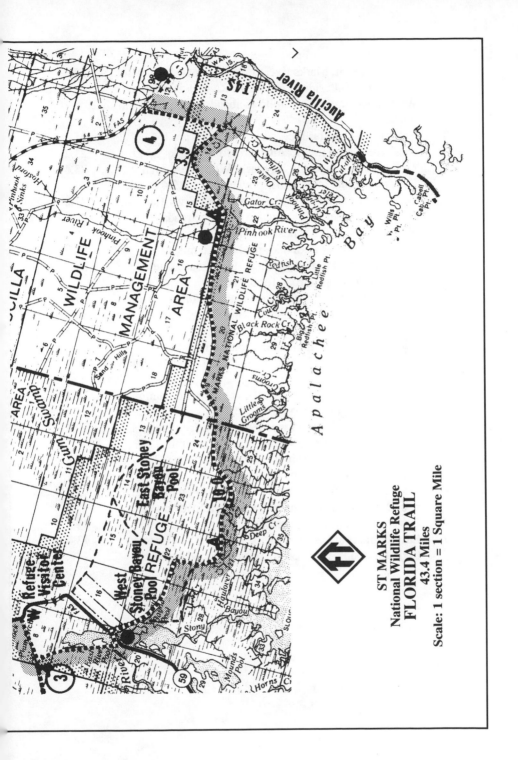

ST MARKS
National Wildlife Refuge
FLORIDA TRAIL
43.4 Miles
Scale: 1 section = 1 Square Mile

Jefferson, Wakulla Counties

19.9	Trail crosses St. Marks river. (Obtain boat ride for safe crossing). South side of St. Marks River is St. Marks Wilderness Area. Trail follows abandoned road for 1.6 miles.	23.5
18.3	Cross Lake Leon bridge.	25.1
18.2	Pass blue-blazed trail leading west to St. Marks River.	25.2
18.0	Trail crosses refuge and St. Marks Wilderness Area. Follows logging road across private land for 2.4 miles.	25.4
15.6	Trail crosses refuge boundary gate. East River Campsite.	27.8
15.5 ③	Trail turns corner at intersection of refuge roads. Pass blue-blazed trail 0.8 miles to Visitor Center. Water. Follow East River Pool dike-road for 1.6 miles.	27.9
13.9	Cross gate at dike-road junction. Lighthouse south 3.6 miles. Follow paved road for 0.4 miles.	29.5
13.5	Cross gate at paved road-dike junction. Follow dike-road for 4.9 miles. Look for otters. Ring Dike Campsite.	29.9
8.6	Trail-grass road junction. West end of swamp-hammock trail. Blue-blazed alternate dry route on road. Trail crosses double pole bridge. Blue-blazed alternate dry route on road.	34.8
5.6	Trail-grass road junction. East end of swamp-hammock trail. Follow graded road for 1.7 miles.	37.8
3.9	Cross Pinhook River on wooden auto bridge. Pinhook River Campsite. Follow grass road for two miles.	39.5
1.9	Trail at grass road terminus. Aucilla Wilderness border.	41.5
1.3	Trail turns sharply north.	42.1
0.7	Trail crosses refuge boundary. Keep west on old road bed. No blazes between terminus and refuge boundary.	42.7
0.1	Cross cable gate and under power lines.	43.3
0.0	East terminus at US 98. Aucilla River 0.75 miles to east. Look for double blaze on south side of road surface.	43.4

Apalachicola National Forest - East

Location
The east part of the Apalachicola forest is located southwest of Tallahassee. The east terminus is on US 319, 1.1 miles west of Medart. The west terminus is at CR 375. Hikers must bypass about a mile of private land on CR 375 and Forest Road 13 to continue on to the west section of the Apalachicola forest trail.

Type of Hiking
The trail goes through swampy forest. Hikers may have to wade after heavy rain. *The water may be waist deep in the Bradwell Bay Wilderness during high water.*

Parking
Park at either terminus at your own risk.

Water
There is no potable water along the trail. Boil, filter or treat all surface water.

Conveniences
Supplies: Sopchoppy, Medart
Mail: Sopchoppy 32358
Motels: Crawfordville
Public Campgrounds: Camel Lake, Hickory Landing, Silver Lake, Wood
        Lake and Wright Lake: all in the National Forest

Emergency
Wakulla County Sheriff: 904-926-7171
Wakulla District Ranger Office: 904-222-9549

Precautions
Wear safety orange if you hike during the general hunting season. Crossing the Bradwell Bay Wilderness through thick titi shrubs requires maps (both FT and USFS) and a compass. Log bridges across Sopchoppy River and Monkey Creek may not be visible in highwater. Check with the U.S. Forest Service before hiking.

Restrictions

Bradwell and Ditch Bays are not suitable for camping. Sopchoppy River and Monkey Creek areas are suitable for camping. Campfires are permitted only in designated areas. For information, write USFS, Wakulla District, Rt. 6, Box 575, Tallahassee 32304.

Description

This trail passes through the eastern part of this 557,000 acre forest through two unique natural features, Bradwell Bay and Ditch Bay. The term "bay" refers to a broad stretch of low land between hills. Bradwell Bay is a huge, shallow saucer containing a vast stretch of titi thicket (buckwheat tree) in the center, with occasional clusters of blackgum and other hardwood trees, surrounded by higher ground with typical pine and palmetto sandy terrain. Bradwell Bay was named for a hunter who was once lost for days in the vast, trackless titi thicket. This wilderness is very similar to the area just to the south called "Tate's Hell" for similar reasons. If the precautions required are taken, the Bays are interesting and beautiful places to hike. The forest sections of this trail contrast with the bays and have a large variety of the plants and animals typical of the pine and palmetto forest. There are orchids, lilies, bladderworts and pitcher plants in addition to oak, maple and gum trees.

Animals of the forest include the red-cockaded woodpecker, osprey and alligator. There are also bald eagles, sandhill cranes, turkeys, bears and panthers. Bee hives filled with titi blossom honey can be seen at the edge of the forest. In the forest look for the scarred pine trees and clay pots which are relics of the turpentine industry. An unusual product of this forest is earthworms, which people harvest by "grunting." Earthworms are called to the surface by driving a wooden stake into the ground and rubbing it with a heavy piece of iron, like a section of steel rail from a railroad scrap pile, to make a "grunting" sound. The young pine plantations of this or any working forest are good places to look for wildlife, because the younger trees produce a higher yield of "mast" (forage foods) per acre than do the older trees. As an interesting side trip after or before a hike, go to the St. Marks lighthouse and the National Wildlife Refuge, just a few miles away on the Gulf of Mexico.

Trail Data - Apalachicola East

Mileage E to W			Mileage W to E
29.0	③	West terminus at paved CR 375. Follow old road.	0.0
25.4		Follow FR 314 for 0.5 mile. Boundary of Bradwell Bay Wilderness. Pass through Bradwell Bay Wilderness. Trail follows north side of Monkey Creek in east half of Wilderness.	3.6
19.0	②	Pass spur trail to parking at FR 329 bridge at Monkey Creek.	10.0
13.5		Trail follows FR 329 for 0.5 mile. Trail follows west side of Sopchoppy River.	15.0
11.3		Cross Monkey Creek on footbridge.	17.7
7.8		Trail crosses Sopchoppy River on forest road bridge.	21.2
7.4		Trail crosses FR 365	21.6
4.4		Cross FR 321.	24.3
4.7		Trail crosses powerline.	24.6
1.0		Cross FR 356. Trail follows jeep trail.	28.0
0.0	①	East terminus at US 319. Look for FT sign. St. Marks section begins 0.3 mile east. Blazes on power poles.	29.0

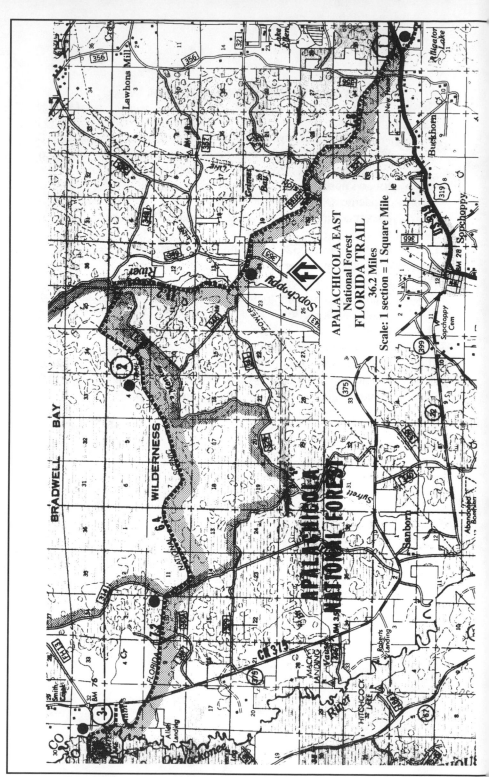

APALACHICOLA EAST
National Forest
FLORIDA TRAIL
36.2 Miles

Scale: 1 section = 1 Square Mile

Wakulla County

Apalachicola National Forest - West

Location
The eastern terminus is on FR 13 at the Ochlockonee River near Porter Lake campground. The western terminus is on CR 12 ten miles south of Bristol.

Type of Hiking
Nearly all the hiking on this trail is over flat, dry pine and palmetto fields with occasional titi swamps. The segment from Memery Island to SR 12 may be ankle-deep in water following heavy rains.

Parking
At the south terminus, park in the Porter Lake campground. At the north terminus, park in the Camel Lake campground.

Water
Potable water is available at Porter Lake and Camel Lake. Boil, filter or treat surface water.

Conveniences
Supplies: Telogia, Bristol
Mail: Bristol 32321
Motel: Bristol
Public Campgrounds: Porter Lake, Camel Lake

Emergency
Liberty County Sheriff: 904-643-5615
Apalachicola District Ranger Office: 904-643-2282

Precautions
Wear safety orange during general hunting season. This area is remote. Carry FT and USFS maps and a compass.

Restrictions
Camp at Porter Lake or Camel Lake during general hunting season. For information, write to USFS, Apalachicola District, P.O. Box 578, Bristol, FL 32321.

Description

This section of the trail crosses the Apalachicola district of the Apalachicola National Forest. The trail passes through and around many large pine palmetto flat woods separated by titi and cypress swamps. The northern end of the trail traverses an interesting low savannah profuse with ground orchids and wild flowers in the spring. Midway along the trail are the remnants of the turpentining settlement of Vilas, a reminder of an era passed. There is good fishing on the Ochlockonee River and in Camel Lake, along with plenty of additional opportunities to fish in the creeks and water holes along the way. This section of trail is one of the most remote in Florida and offers a wide variety of flora and fauna year-round. Carry a compass and the National Forest map. The trail is marked on the National Forest map.

Trail Data - Apalachicola West

Mileage E to W		Mileage W to E
33.4	West terminus at CR 12 10 miles south of Bristol.	0.0
30.2	At Memery Island pass 3.5 mile blue-blazed trail to Hidden Pond.	3.2
28.4 ③	Cross FR 105. Camel Lake Campground 0.1 mile west.	5.0
26.6	Trail crosses Big Gully Creek on FR 105.	6.8
24.9	FT junction with FR 108 at woods around Hidden Pond. Trail meets blue-blazed 3.5 mile trail to Memery Island.	8.5
23.9	Trail crosses private property for 0.2 miles. Follows woods road and FR 108.	9.5
21.5	Cross over creek on FR 112-H.	11.9
18.6	Trail junction with FR 112. Use cattle-proof opening in fence. Follow FR 112.	14.8
18.1 ②	Turn at FR 112-SR 65 junction. Follow SR 65 over the New River. Follow FR 120.	15.3
17.9	Cross railroad tracks on FR 120.	15.5
16.5	Trail leaves road and enters woods.	16.9
15.9	Trail junction with FR 107. Follow FR 107 for 0.6 miles.	17.5
15.3	Trail junction with FR 107.	18.1
13.9	Cross FR 107-B.	19.5
9.9	Cross FR 175.	23.5
9.0	Trail junction with FR 107. Follow FR 107 for 2.2 miles.	24.4
6.8	Trail junction with FR 107.	26.6
6.1	Cross FR 177.	27.3
4.8	Cross Indian Creek on CR 67.	28.6
4.4	Cross Indian Creek bridge.	29.0
3.3	Cross over creek on FR 142.	30.1
2.1	Enter circular clearing.	31.3
0.8	Cross FH 13.	32.6
0.0 ①	East terminus at FH 13 Ochlockonee River bridge near Porter Lake Campground.	33.4

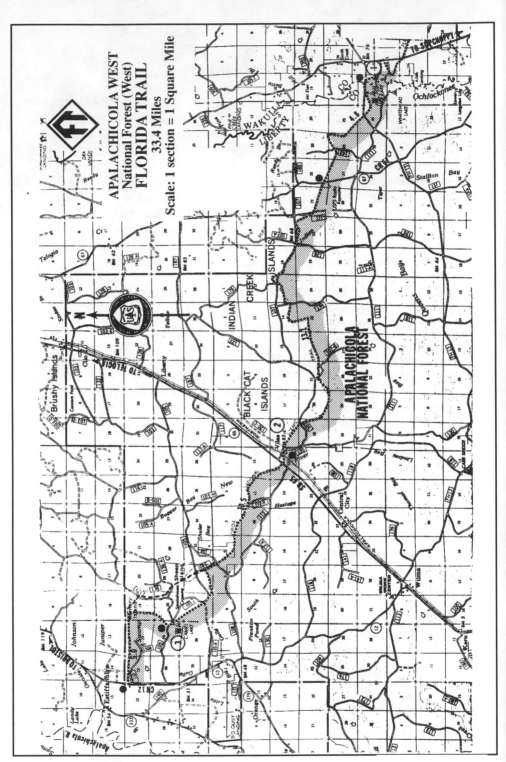

APALACHICOLA WEST
National Forest (West)
FLORIDA TRAIL
33.4 Miles
Scale: 1 section = 1 Square Mile

Liberty County

Torreya State Park

Location
Torreya State Park is 12 miles north of Bristol near Rock Bluff on CR 271. Enter the park via CR 270 or CR 271 from SR 12 between Bristol and Greensboro.

Type of Hiking
The terrain in this region is "mountainous," with real cliffs. Its flora and topography are unique. Both overnight and day hikes are possible.

Parking
Park at the park entrance, the picnic area and the Gregory House.

Water
Potable water is available at the Gregory House, the campground, the picnic area and the front entrance parking lot.

Conveniences
Supplies: Bristol
Mail: Bristol 32321
Motels: Bristol
Public Campgrounds: In the park

Emergency
Liberty County Sheriff: 904-643-3532
Park Manager: 904-643-2674

Precautions
Park is open from 8 a.m. to sundown. Plan hiking to suit these hours. The trail is blazed white. There is a fee for primitive camping. Check in with the ranger at the Gregory House. For information, write to Superintendent, Rt. 2, Box 70, Bristol, FL 32321.

Restrictions
All plant and animal life is protected; do not disturb plants and animals in the park. Small fires are permitted only in camping areas. Fires are prohibited in times of drought.

Description

Torreya State Park is one of the most unusual in the state, resembling trails in the Appalachian mountains more than semi-tropical trails. The Torreya perimeter trail, a loop of about seven miles, traverses ravines and streams and bluffs which rise over 150 feet above the Apalachicola River. Logan's Bluff towers to about 300 feet. Forests of the park include the river swamp, hardwood hammocks and high pine-land. Each of these communities has a different set of trees, shrubs, and wildflowers.

Look for the rare Florida yew tree (the largest bigleaf magnolia in the U.S.), dogwood, yellow jasmine, azalea, and the gopherwood or "stinking cedar," from which Noah is supposed to have constructed the Ark. The Torreya tree found here grows only in this location. Wildlife is common and includes deer, beaver, bobcat, gray fox, the rare Barbour's map turtle and over 100 species of birds.

This park is historically significant. Traces of the Indians who lived here still remain. There were Confederate gun batteries here during the Civil War. Look for the ruins of the emplacements near the bluffs overlooking the Apalachicola. The ranger's station is in the historic Gregory plantation house, which was restored after it was moved to Torreya. Stop here before hiking for help in identifying the unique plants along the trail.

Trail Data - Torreya

Mileage Counterclockwise		Mileage Clockwise
	Terminus at parking lot. Follow blue-blazed 0.6 mile access trail, south end of parking lot.	
6.1	Junction of main loop and access trail.	0.0
6.0	Pass Rock Creek campsite 250 yards north on white-blazed trail. Trail passes along streams and over hills for 0.7 miles.	0.1
5.3	Trail junction with woods road. Follow road over bridge for 0.5 miles.	0.8
4.8	Trail junction with road.	1.3
3.4	Cross park entrance road.	2.7
3.0	Pass Red Rock scenic vista. Cliffs: use caution.	3.1
2.3	Trail junction with old road. Trail follows old road for 0.3 miles.	3.8
1.9	Pass River Bluffs primitive campsite, pit toilet.	4.2

0.9	Junction with unmarked Indian Relics Trail leading to parking lot.	5.2
0.8	Junction with Gregory Mansion side trail. Trail passes along Apalachicola River bluff for 0.2 miles	5.3
0.3	Junction with Gregory Mansion side trail.	5.8
0.0	Junction of main loop and access trail. Follow 0.6 miles blue-blazed access trail at south end of parking lot.	6.1

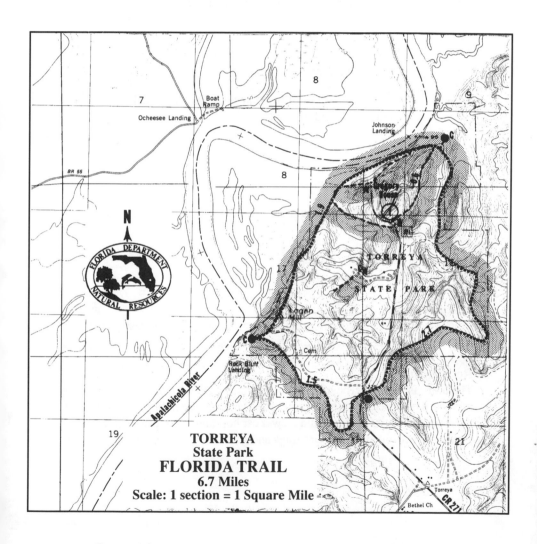

TORREYA
State Park
FLORIDA TRAIL
6.7 Miles
Scale: 1 section = 1 Square Mile

Liberty County

Pine Log

Location
The western terminus is at the Choctawhatchee River on SR 20 near Ebro.

Type of Hiking
The hiking on this trail is mostly on flat terrain, passing cypress-lined lakes on woods trails, and using forest roads through silvaculture areas. Stream crossings and low areas may require wading after heavy rains.

Parking
Park at the Pine Log Environmental Center in the State Forest.

Water
Potable water is available at the Environmental Center. Creek and surface water must be boiled, filtered or treated.

Conveniences
Supplies: Ebro
Mail: Ebro 32437
Motels: Panama City
Public Campgrounds: Pine Log State Forest (with showers)

Emergency
Bay County Sheriff: 904-785-4351
Division of Forestry: 904-872-4175

Precautions
Pine Log State Forest does not take camping reservations. Forestry practices may alter trail markings. Use a map and compass.

Restrictions
The trail east of SR 79 (beyond the loop at mile 4.1) is closed to hikers the first nine days of general hunting season, the Thanksgiving holiday weekend and the week between Chrismas and New Year holidays. Campfires in the State Forest are permitted only in fire rings and grills at the Environmental Center.

Description

This trail skirts the sand hills region and traverses pine flatwoods. The sand hills are relics of old dunes. Low areas are dominated by titi and cypress while higher areas are used for pine silvaculture. The 6,911- acre State Forest features a swimming lake, and lakes for canoeing and fishing. Hawks and owls can be seen hunting over the grasses and shrubs of recent clearcuts or newly planted areas. Herds of deer frequent the dense hardwood undergrowth of older areas.

Trail Data - Pine Log

Mileage E to W		Mileage W to E
8.8	West terminus at Choctawhatchee River bridge on SR 20 at Ebro.	0.0
7.9	Trail route turns at SR 20 intersection with north-south road.	0.9
7.4	Trail junction with north-south road south of SR 20.	1.4
6.9	Cross north boundary of Pine Log State Forest. Trail crosses two forest roads.	1.9
5.7	Junction with 2.1 mile white-blazed loop trail (see map inset).	3.1
5.3	Trail junction with short spur trail to campground, lakes.	3.5
4.8	Junction with 2.1 mile white-blazed loop trail (see map inset).	4.0
4.7	Trail junction with SR 79. Route follows SR 79. Cross Pine Log Creek on SR 79 bridge.	4.1
4.5	Trail junction with SR 79 just south of bridge.	4.3
3.7	Route skirts north edge of savannah. Trail follows Pine Log Creek floodplain line crossing several infrequently flooded titi streams.	5.1
1.5	Cross Ditch Branch on log bridge.	7.3
0.0	East terminus at boundary of Pine Log State Forest.	8.8

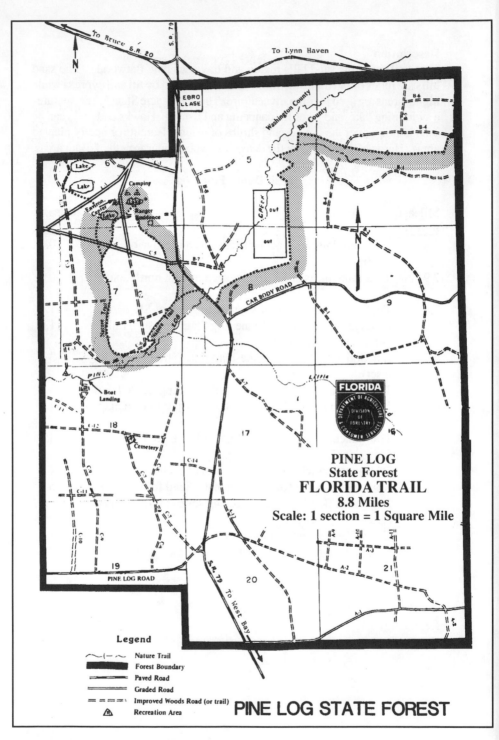

Legend

~(–~   Nature Trail
▬▬▬   Forest Boundary
═══   Paved Road
───   Graded Road
= = =   Improved Woods Road (or trail)
Ⓐ   Recreation Area

PINE LOG STATE FOREST

PINE LOG
State Forest
FLORIDA TRAIL
8.8 Miles
Scale: 1 section = 1 Square Mile

Bay County

Jackson Red Ground Trail

Location
The trail is northwest of Crestview in the Blackwater River State Forest. The north-eastern terminus is at Karick Lake Recreation Area off CR 189, three miles south of Blackman. The southwestern terminus is at Red Rock picnic area, 3.7 miles east from the Spring Hill Church sign, which is 12.5 miles north of Milton on SR 191.

Type of Hiking
The trail offers 21.5 miles of slightly hilly hiking through pine and hardwood forest. A 4.5 mile side trail to Krul recreation area provides a shorter forest hike.

Parking
Park at Karick Lake, Red Rock, and the Krul recreation area.

Water
Potable water is available at Karick Lake, at the Krul recreation area, and at the Bear recreation area. Boil, filter or treat river, stream and ground water.

Conveniences
Supplies: Baker
Mail: Baker 32531
Motels: Milton, Crestview
Public Campgrounds: Krul and Bear Lake recreation areas

Emergency
Santa Rosa County Sheriff: 904-623-3691
Okaloosa County Sheriff: 904-682-7288
Division of Forestry: 904-957-4201

Precautions
Obtain information from State Forest Headquarters, Rt. 1, Box 77, Milton, FL 32570. Phone: 904-957-4201

Restrictions
Camp only at designated sites. Campfires are permitted only at the two shelters, and at the end points.

Description

This trail, named for the red soil of the area, is in the 183,153-acre Blackwater River State Forest, Florida's largest state forest. The Blackwater, Coldwater, and Sweetwater Juniper Rivers are clean, sandy-bottom, spring-fed waters, in spite of the dark coloring imparted by tannin from the river bank cypress. A wide range of flora and fauna flourishes along the trail. Pines and junipers predominate, but there are also oak, cypress, ash, live oak, tupelo, bay, and wax myrtle trees, as well as holly, pyracantha, titi and youpon shrubs. Blueberries and blackberries can be picked in early summer. In the fall, the hardwood foliage changes color, and although the hues are not as brilliant as on the Appalachian Trail, the display is well worth seeing. Raccoons, beavers, deer, rabbits, foxes, bobcats, and most other Florida animals live here, as do ospreys, wood ducks, herons and eagles. There are places to swim along this trail.

The trail retraces one of the earliest trade routes of Indians and settlers in Florida. It was used by General Andrew Jackson on his second trip to Florida in 1818. Jackson marched 1,200 men from the Apalachicola River to Pensacola in 18 days.

Trail Data - Jackson Red Ground

Mileage S to N		Mileage N to S
	Terminus at SE corner of Karick Lake. Camping, water, latrines. Fires permitted here.	
21.5 ①	Trail follows along earthen dam. Trail follows along lake. Pass park restroom and picnic area.	0.0
20.9	Hills and swamp-stream areas. Trail passes through oaks.	0.6
19.7	Cross CR 189. Change elevation through pine forest.	1.8
17.7	Cross ravine on clay road bridge. Trail passes through planted pine grove. Trail passes through off-road hills and marshes.	3.8
14.8	Trail follows clay road.	6.7
14.5	Junction of clay roads. Watch blazes. Trail follows clay road.	7.0
13.6	Junction of clay roads. Cross Blackwater River on bridge. Trail follows clay road through swamp.	7.9

JACKSON RED GROUND
Blackwater River State Forest
FLORIDA TRAIL
21.5 Miles
Scale: 1 section = 1 Square Mile

Okaloosa, Santa Rosa Counties

12.5	Cross stream. If water is high, a better crossing is downstream at log track.	9.0
12.0	Shelter in dense trees. Fires permitted here.	9.5
11.6	Cross stream on foot bridge.	9.9
10.2	Cross stream on railroad ties.	11.3
9.6	Cross paved road. Change elevation. Cross small stream. Change elevation. Several sharp turns through pines.	11.9
8.1	Cross stream on hand bridge in forest. Follow clay road.	13.4
8.0	Trail turns sharp (north-south).	13.5
7.6	Pass Santa Rosa-Okaloosa County line sign.	13.9
7.1	Sweetwater Trail junction to north, crosses Highway four.	14.4
6.4	Cross paved road.	15.1
6.1	Shelter on west side of trail. Campfires permitted here. Trail follows clay road, changes elevation.	15.4
5.1	Trail passes through mature pine forest.	16.4
1.6	Cross clay road. Trail passes through hardwood swamp.	19.9
0.3	Trail follows clay road.	21.2
0.0 ②	Terminus at bridge across creek. Red Rock picnic area at Juniper Creek. Fires permitted here.	21.5

The Perfect Blaze

The perfect blaze is two inches by six inches with straight sides and square corners painted on a plane at right angles to the direction of the trail six feet above the ground.

Bob Atwater
Trailmaster

BUILDING THE FLORIDA TRAIL

Trail development is complicated. Each section of the Florida Trail system results from hundreds of hours of volunteer work. Fortunately, this work tends to be the most comradely and interesting aspect of the Association's activities. Hiking a section of trail on which one has worked is especially satisfying. Following is a brief description of how a section is developed, constructed and maintained with the help of FTA members. Information on trail development is given in the FTA Trail Manual, available from FTA headquarters. Volunteer help is always welcome.

Decision to Proceed
Based on recommendations from members, the FTA Board decides when resources should be committed to develop a section of trail.

Study
Aerial photos and topographical maps are obtained (usually at the county courthouse). A tentative route is laid out that offers dry hiking in most seasons, best views, shade, fewest stream crossings, and good camp sites.

Ownership Search
Volunteers then go to the county courthouse with the proposed route. It is checked against the tax rolls to identify the owners of land through which the trail would pass. These are noted on the topographic map. The tax rolls are also used to get the names and addresses of the owners.

Negotiations
The landowners are contacted by letter or, preferably, personally by an FTA member. The objectives of the trail and the FTA are explained, and a request is made to cross the owner's land with the trail. The landowner's concerns about such things as liability are addressed. If the owner agrees, an agreement is signed which includes any restrictions or requirements specified by the landowner. Land owners may obtain certain tax advantages when conservation easements are made for the trail.

Trail Layout
Volunteers traverse the area, selecting the most desirable footpath and marking it with orange surveyor's tape. This route is marked on the topographic map. It is reviewed with the owner, to show precisely what is planned. If the owner approves, the trail is constructed.

Trail Construction
Work parties of volunteers are organized, each under leadership of an experienced trail builder. Work hikes are announced in the FTA newsletter. These parties may either hike by day and camp overnight near their vehicles, or backpack and camp along the trail. They will clear brush, build bridges and paint blazes until the trail is completed. This may require many weekends of work. Good times and conversations around the campfire after a day of trail work are among the best memories of FTA members After a trail is finished, the data and rough layouts are given to the FTA cartographer, who prepares maps for the guide books.

Trail Maintenance
The FTA is responsible for maintaining the trail, for re-routing it if required, and for assuring that a good relationship is maintained with the host landowner. Periodic work hikes are scheduled to maintain the trail.

FTA Membership
Membership in the Florida Trail Association provides opportunities to build and maintain the Florida Trail System, hike on the entire trail system including the trails on private property, and participate in other activities. The guide book to the complete trail, *Walking the Florida Trail*, is available to members only.

Members get the bimonthly newsletter, the *Footprint*, which includes trail news, changes and updates to the entire trail system, and news of the more than 500 hikes and activities scheduled throughout the year. State and regional conferences are held and include training sessions in trail building, leading activities, backpacking, orienteering and nature programs.

The local FTA chapters allow members to share transportation to activities, to meet hiking and canoeing partners and to help maintain a nearby section of trail. A portion of FTA dues goes to the local chapter to be used for regional newsletters, trail maintenance, equipment, etc.

To join, write or call:
>Florida Trail Association
>P.O. Box 13708
>Gainesville, FL 32604
>1-800-343-1882 (toll-free in Florida only)
>904-378-8823

Bibliography

Keller, John M. and Ernest A. Baldini. *Walking the Florida Trail.*
    Gainesville, FL: Florida Trail Association, Inc., 1985.

The Woodlands Post, A Quarterly Journal of Florida Forestry.
    Tallahassee, FL: Florida Department of Agriculture and Consumer
    Services Division of Forestry.

Florida Canoe and Hiking Trails in State Forests. U.S. Forest Service, P. O.
    Box 13549, Tallahassee, FL 32302.

Brochures and Maps of Hiking Trails in State Forests.   State Forest
    Headquarters, Collins Bldg., Tallahassee, FL 32304.

Topographical Maps. Branch of Distribution, U.S. Geological Survey,
    1200 Eads St., Arlington, VA 2202.

Florida County Maps. Florida Department of Transportation, 605
    Suwannee St., Tallahassee, FL 32304.

Further Reading

Backpacking, Hiking, Walking:

The Complete Walker I, II, and III, Colin Fletcher.

Backpacking, R. C. Rethmel.

The Basic Essentials of Women in the Outdoors, Judith Niemi.

A Woman's Journey (an Account of the Apalachian Trail), Cindy Ross.

A Walk Across America, and*Walk to the West,* Peter Jenkins.

Backpacking One Step at a Time, Harvey Manning.

Camping and Cooking:

The Well-Fed Backpacker, June Fleming.

Backpacker's Recipe Book: Inexpensive Gourmet Cooking for the Backpacker,
    Steve Antell.

Camping Secrets: A Lexicon of Camping Tips Only the Experts Know, Cliff
    Jacobson.

Family and Kids:

Sharing Nature With Children and *Sharing the Joy of Nature*, Joseph Cornell.

Starting Small in the Wilderness, The Sierra Club Outdoors Guide for Families.

Nature:

Reading the Woods, Vinson Brown.

The New Wilderness Handbook , Paul Petzoldt with Raye Carleson Ringholz.

Soft Paths: How to Enjoy the Wilderness Without Harming It, Bruce Hampton and David Cole.

Walking Softly in the Wilderness, The Sierra Club.

Florida:

Side Roads of Florida, James Warnke.

Florida Parks: A Guide to Camping in Nature, Gerald Grow.

A Canoeing and Kayaking Guide to the Streams of Florida, Vols. 1 and 2, Elizabeth F. Carter and John L. Pearce.

Florida Off the Beaten Path, A Guide to Unique Places, Diana and Gill Gleasner.

A Hiking Guide to the Trails of Florida, Elizabeth F. Carter.

Wilderness Survival:

Surviving the Unexpected Wilderness Emergency, Gene Feas.

Standard First Aid and Personal Safety, The American Red Cros.s

Plants that Poison, Ervin M. Schmutz, Ph.D. and Lucretia Breazeale Hamilton.

Field Guide to Edible Wild Plants, Bradford Angier.

Wilderness Medicine, William Forgey, M.D.

How to Stay Alive in the Woods, Bradford Angier.

INDEX

hurricane, 26, 140
hypothermia, 10

I
Indians, 37, 41, 69, 109, 135, 141, 156, 162
    Miccosukee, 22, 23
    Timucuan, 111
infection, 10
insects, 8-9
ivory-billed woodpecker, 11

J
Jackson Red Ground Trail, 161
Jonathan Dickinson State Park Trail, 44

K
Kern, Jim, vii
Kissimmee River Trail, 54

L
Lake Arbuckle Trail, 79
Lake Kissimmee State Park Trail, 83
lightning, 9
Little Manatee River State Recreation Area Trail, 86
logging, 45, 65, 94, 142
Lyme disease, 9

M
map and compass, 1
mining, 88, 89
mink, 16
mixed hardwood/pine forests, 14
munitions, 54, 79
Myakka River Trail, 48

N
National Forests
    Apalachicola - East, 147
    Apalachicola - West, 151
    Ocala - North, 118

Ocala - South, 114
Osceola, 126
night hiking, 8
North Florida, 109

O
Ocala Trail, 114, 118
Okeechobee Trail, 25, 30
old-growth, 111
organizing pack, 4
Osceola Trail, 126
otters, 16, 130

P
Panhandle, 135
parking, 1
pets, 2
Pine Log Trail, 158
pine flatwoods, 12
pioneers, 49
poisonous plants, 9
Prairie Lakes Trail, 58
problems and precautions, 7

R
railroad, 142
red-cockaded woodpecker, 14, 37
registers, 1
Richloam Trail, 98
roseate spoonbill, 12
royal palm, 22, 23

S
salt evaporation, 141, 142
salt marsh snake, 16
salt marshes, 16
sand pine scrub, 15
sandhill community, 14
sandhill crane, 12, 16, 35, 49, 55, 59, 80, 84
scrub cypress, 12
Seminole Ranch Trail, 74
shelter, 3

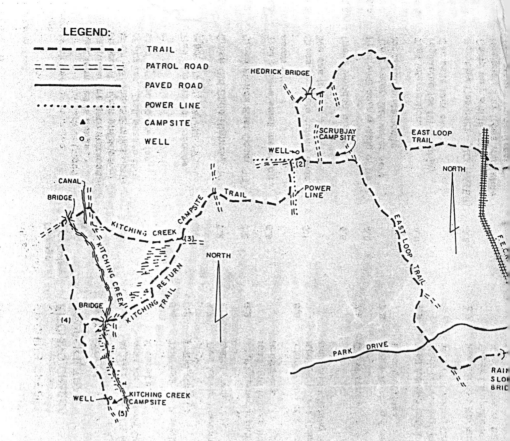

LEGEND:

- – – – – – TRAIL
- ≡ ≡ ≡ ≡ ≡ PATROL ROAD
- ───────── PAVED ROAD
- · · · · · · POWER LINE
- ▲ CAMPSITE
- ○ WELL

HEDRICK BRIDGE

SCRUBJAY CAMPSITE

EAST LOOP TRAIL

WELL

(2)

POWER LINE

NORTH

CANAL

BRIDGE

KITCHING CREEK TRAIL

CAMPSITE

(3)

NORTH

EAST LOOP TRAIL

KITCHING CREEK

KITCHING RETURN TRAIL

BRIDGE

(4)

PARK DRIVE

RAIN SLOUGH BRIDGE

WELL

KITCHING CREEK CAMPSITE

(5)

F E C

- The value in this land is not only your enjoyment but also in leaving no trace of your visit.

- Please pack out your trash and that left behind by others.

- If you smoke, please stop to find a safe place to extinguish your cigarette, and take the butt and any expended matches with you.

- Please take only pictures, leave only footprints.

THE FLORIDA N.

When completel
Scenic Trail, the
from the Gulf Is
sacola to the
Preserve near N
than 1,300 miles
for educational r

How can YOU
Resou

— Join the Flori

— Volunteer to
portion of the
"Trail Krewe"

— Contribute m
help support

— Become an ac
about this imp

Blazes on trees and posts mark the route of the trails. Two blazes generally designate a change in direction. Carefully locate the next blaze after a double blaze before continuing.

Jonathan Dickinson State Park

Hiking Trails

Florida Trail
ASSOCIATION
E.M.C.

P.O. BOX 13708 GAINESVILLE, FLORIDA 32604
(904) 378-8823
1-800-343-1882

JONATHAN DICKINSON STATE PARK
16450 SE Federal Highway
Hobe Sound, Florida 33455
(407) 546-2771

Prepared by
Loxahatchee Chapter, FTA
P.O. Box 19393
West Palm Beach
FL 33416-9393
(407) 967-1346

INTRACOASTAL WATERWAY

HOBE SOUND

(U.S. HWY #1)

ENTRANCE STATION
AND PARKING LOT

LAKE

TIONAL SCENIC TRAIL

certified as a National
Florida Trail will meander
and Seashore near Pen-
Big Cypress National
ami and Naples. More
of a preserved resource
creation.

**help build a National
ce in Florida?**

a Trail Association.

help build and maintain a
Florida Trail by joining a
n your area.

ney and other property to
is effort.

ive citizen by telling others
rtant wilderness resource.